NOMOS
GLASHÜTTE

'n support of

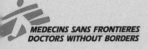
**MÉDECINS SANS FRONTIERES
DOCTORS WITHOUT BORDERS**

D1166012

GRANTA

12 Addison Avenue, London W11 4QR | email editorial@granta.com
To subscribe go to granta.com, or call 020 8955 7011 (free phone 0500 004 033)
in the United Kingdom, 845-267-3031 (toll-free 866-438-6150) in the United States

ISSUE 135: SPRING 2016

This selection copyright © 2016 Granta Publications.

Granta, ISSN 173231, is published four times a year by Granta Publications, 12 Addison Avenue, London W11 4QR, United Kingdom.

The US annual subscription price is $48. Airfreight and mailing in the USA by agent named Air Business Ltd, c/o Worldnet-Shipping USA Inc., 156−15 146th Avenue, 2nd Floor, Jamaica, NY 11434, USA. Periodicals postage paid at Jamaica, NY 11431.

US Postmaster: Send address changes to *Granta*, Air Business Ltd, c/o Worldnet-Shipping USA Inc., 156−15 146th Avenue, 2nd Floor, Jamaica, NY 11434, USA.

Subscription records are maintained at *Granta*, c/o Abacus e-Media, Chancery Exchange, 10 Furnival Street, London EC4A 1YH.

Air Business Ltd is acting as our mailing agent.

Granta is printed and bound in Italy by Legoprint. This magazine is printed on paper that fulfils the criteria for 'Paper for permanent document' according to ISO 9706 and the American Library Standard ANSI/NIZO Z39.48-1992 and has been certified by the Forest Stewardship Council (FSC). *Granta* is indexed in the American Humanities Index.

ISBN 978-1-905-881-95-6

National
Portrait
Gallery

RUSSIA AND THE ARTS

THE AGE OF TOLSTOY AND TCHAIKOVSKY

A once-in-a-lifetime
opportunity to see
masterpieces from
the State Tretyakov
Gallery in Moscow

NOW OPEN
UNTIL 26 JUNE 2016

BOOK NOW
npg.org.uk/russia

Free for Members

Creative Writing at Royal Holloway

MA in Creative Writing
Practice-based PhD programme

Royal Holloway, University of London offers one of the most vibrant and successful Creative Writing programmes in the UK.

The MA in Creative Writing is based at our London campus, 11 Bedford Square in Bloomsbury. With courses taught by Jo Shapcott, Susanna Jones, Kei Miller, Benjamin Markovits, Nikita Lalwani, Redell Olsen and others, as well as a number of visiting professors, you will join a community of inspiring authors of international standing.

Many of our MA Creative Writing and PhD students have gone on to critical success; from publishing novels and collections of poetry, to nominations for and winning major literary awards.

 For more information on postgraduate courses email lisa.dacunha@royalholloway.ac.uk
Royal Holloway, University of London, Egham, Surrey TW20 0EX

royalholloway.ac.uk/creativewritingprogrammes @rhulenglish

International
Literature
Festival
Dublin

You complete the story

International Literature Festival Dublin 2016
May 21–29

ilfdublin.com

Comhairle Cathrach
Bhaile Átha Cliath
Dublin City Council

GRAVEYARD CLAY *CRÉ NA CILLE*

MÁIRTÍN Ó CADHAIN

Translated by Liam Mac Con Iomaire
and Tim Robinson

In critical opinion and popular polls, Máirtín Ó Cadhain's
Graveyard Clay is invariably ranked the most important
prose work in modern Irish. This bold new translation
of his radically original *Cré na Cille* is the shared project
of two fluent speakers of the Irish of Ó Cadhain's native
region, Liam Mac Con Iomaire and Tim Robinson.
They have achieved a lofty goal: to convey Ó Cadhain's
meaning accurately and to meet his towering literary
standards.

Graveyard Clay is a novel of black humour, reminiscent
of the work of Synge and Beckett. This edition of
Ó Cadhain's masterpiece is enriched with footnotes,
bibliography, publication and reception history, and
other materials that invite further study and deeper
enjoyment of his most engaging and challenging work.

6 b/w illustrations Hardback £16.99

More literature in translation from the Margellos World Republic of Letters

After the Circus	The Hatred of Music	Orthokostá	The Roar of Morning	The Walnut Mansion
A Novel	Pascal Quignard	*A Novel*	Tip Marugg	Miljenko Jergović
Patrick Modiano	Translated by	Thanassis Valtinos	Translated by	Translated by
Translated by	Matthew Amos	Translated by	Paul Vincent	Stephen M. Dickey, wit
Mark Polizzotti	& Fredrik Rönnbäck	Jane Assimakopoulos	**Paperback £10.99**	Janja Pavetić-Dickey
Paperback £10.99	**Hardback £16.99**	& Stavros Deligiorgis		**Hardback £17.99**
		Hardback £16.99		

YaleBooks | tel: 020 7079 4900
www.yalebooks.co.uk

CONTENTS

Introduction

We started working on this issue over a year ago, and we have rarely read as widely and as deeply for any country issue as we have for this. Many things that we loved didn't make it in – you could fill volumes with contemporary Irish writing of exceptional quality, and space, as ever, was limited.

People ask me what, if anything, defines Irish writing. We have seen some trends – one editor wrote about perceiving a sense of displacement, and the ability of our authors to capture the inflections of various dialects. Someone else talked about seeing a fraught relationship between place and self. We are conscious, of course, of Ireland's bleak history, and Britain's role in it, but the nature of the relationship between people and land also has a modern reincarnation in the markedly international nature of Irish writers. They are closer to America than British writers tend to be, both linguistically and geographically, but they are also closer to Europe. The authors in this issue live or have lived in many different countries, and there is an Irish diaspora vaster by far than the population of Ireland – some 80 million people around the world are said to identify as Irish.

We did worry that perhaps our photoessays might seem objectifying – the rough youth; the sectarianism in the north; the beauty of the Travellers. But Ireland is Ireland. It resists and relishes its own national images in equal measure. It's true, also, that the oblique subject matter of most of the stories in this collection is really Ireland itself. Colm Tóibín's story, set in Berlin, is one exception. Almost every other writer in the issue, from Kevin Barry to Roddy Doyle, from Sara Baume to Colin Barrett, engages with some degree of inner dialogue about Irishness, as though that condition itself is not a neutral, or a given, but, rather like Israeli or Russian nationhood, an existential state of being associated with certain traits and traditions.

Emma Donoghue engages with the church and rural poverty. Her nineteenth-century narrator, an English nurse, comments freely on the queasy phenomenon of a starving Irish miracle child in a poor cottage. Belinda McKeon's story, 'Party, Party', can be read as an allegory of modern Ireland, with its references to the famous Arlo, who may or may not turn up for the party, and the child who learns to sing for money in 'the old language, the lovely one'. The question of Ireland, of the church and sexuality, is there in Roddy Doyle's description of Brother Murphy, a teacher, whose words to a boy of thirteen, 'Victor Forde, I can never resist your smile,' come to haunt both teacher and child – 'he fuckin' fancies him,' Victor's friend Derek Mullally whispers. Ireland is there in the references to pregnancy and abortion; to crime; to drugs; to gangs; to the green fields beyond the cities and the housing developments.

Irish writers, we hear, are tired of the question of why there are so many good Irish writers now; the question of the Irish 'literary boom'. Editors coin these phrases of course, but we now believe it to be true: there is something about Irish writing that really is exceptional.

Why? Many reasons, but not least language – writers like to twist and turn it to see what it can do. Irish writers have a wealth of religious and revolutionary codes and cadences to draw from; they have the Gaelic of Irish, and the strange and potent Travellers' Shelta, or the Cant, Gammon or Tarri. John Connell, in this issue, quotes the Lord's Prayer in Gammon: '*Our gathra, who cradgies in the manyak-norch,*' it begins. '*We turry kerrath about your moniker.*' I think of *Finnegans Wake*, of *A Clockwork Orange* and of *1984*. What does Gammon sound like? Who knows. But I like it.

We commissioned acclaimed photographer Eamonn Doyle for our author photographs. They are, I hope you agree, dramatic and interesting, giving a sense of streets and landscapes as well as characters.

Finally, I want to thank Chris Agee, Sinéad Gleeson, Lucy Luck, Declan Meade and John O'Brien – your help and support have been invaluable. ■

Sigrid Rausing

THE RAINGOD'S GREEN, DARK AS PASSION

Kevin Barry

1

If cities are sexed, as Jan Morris believes, then Cork is a male place. Personified further, I would cast him as low-sized, disputatious and stoutly built, a hard-to-knock-over type. He has a haughty demeanour that's perhaps not entirely earned but he can also, in a kinder light, seem princely. He is certainly melancholic. He is given to surreal flights and to an antic humour and he is blessed with pleasingly musical speech patterns. He is careful with money. He is in most leanings a liberal. He is fairly cool, usually quite relaxed, and head over heels in love with himself.

At the very least, the last of this is true: the city of Cork is besotted with itself, and it talks of little else. Quite right, too – it's a gorgeous place, it's enormous fun, and it has an operatic atmosphere. By operatic, I mean that its passions are fervently held and fervently debated, and there is a native tendency to melodrama: the hand gestures are near-Italianate. I lived in the city from my early twenties until my early thirties – it is in many ways responsible for the creature that I have become, and I hold no rancour against it for this. In fact, though it's a decade and a half since I lived there, when I go back to visit now it still feels a bit like going home.

2

I had maybe a dozen addresses in Cork. I can walk them in my mind, from attic flat to terrace house to glorified bedsit, and I see that they trace out a rough perimeter of the city centre. Cork is compact but a little confusing – it seems to circle back on itself around the quays of the Lee river. Much of the centre of town is built inside a loop of the river. You're forever crossing little bridges over the river only to arrive at another little bridge over the same river. It would be rare to see the Lee in a mad rush to get anywhere. It seems happy enough to saunter slowly through the streets of the place in a Cork accent. Once I saw a woman try to drown herself in it. She walked down the steps of the river wall at George's Quay. It was early in the evening and it was quiet around the streets – maybe it was a Sunday. It was the summertime. We were on Father Matthew Quay, across the river, and we called out to her but she didn't seem to hear us. That it was in daylight the scene played out made it even more disturbing. She hesitated as the water lapped at her ankles – she lurched forward, but she relented again and caught herself. We ran across the bridge. We called to her again. Others who were passing by called to her, too. At last she visibly buckled, as though she'd been struck a blow; she sat down on the stone steps, and the river moved slowly past, regardless. After a short while an ambulance came and the medics fetched the woman tenderly up from the river wall and she was helped away. Maybe the river had spoken to her. Maybe it said –You're kidding me. You'd leave Cork?

3

It is built on a marsh and it has a dampness that enters the bones. This has a tendency to turn one both tubercular and poetical. On the Ballyhooly Road I used to put on two extra jumpers to go to bed. I was in a back bedroom of what was at one time a farmhouse, before the suburbs engulfed this area just south of Mayfield. There were huge hooks hanging from the kitchen ceiling to keep the hams up away from the animals. There was a rat behind the wainscotting still

– we named him Frank after the Irish for a rat, 'an Francach', which means, literally, 'a Frenchman'. Frank was a very scratchy customer late on in the evening, until we poisoned him.

It was a fine house in the summer but a nightmare in the winter. Five or six of us shared it at any one time – the place was huge. My bedroom looked out over the Glen, a surviving expanse of countryside nestled into the north side of the city. It was a metropolis of notably scrawny rabbits and lads used to hunt them by night in specially adapted vehicles (most often old Volkswagen Beetles) with high-powered headlamps and an extra seat strapped to the bonnet for the shooter. This practice was known as 'lamping' and it was scored competitively. Cork was a city of strange fraternities. I'd lie there in the winter nights and listen to the gunshot blasts and watch the icicles form inside my window frame. There was no central heating. I had sleeping bags, blankets and coats mounted a foot thick on top of me. I was determined to be to Cork what Saul Bellow had been to Chicago but it wasn't working out so well. Not least, perhaps, because of the amount of hash I was smoking.

But there was a tang in the atmosphere of the city that made you want to create something in answer to it. The place felt closed-in, enveloping and somehow unpredictable. Paul Durcan described Cork's feeling well when he wrote that it was 'as intimate and homicidal as a Little Marseilles'.

4

Once on a summer night from that same bedroom I heard a woman sing after midnight in a garden. I didn't recognise or don't remember the song but her voice was extraordinarily sweet as it came up from the darkness, and it caused a great hush of feeling in the gathering that she was a part of. I lay on the bed with the window open to the summer night – I was as rapturously lonesome as you can be only in your mid-twenties – and I listened to the song and I was so moved I tried to communicate messages by means of telepathy to a girl who was at that moment sleeping across the city. This didn't work out so well either.

5

There is a sense when you're in Cork that the rest of the world is receding. Oh it's still out there, somewhere, in the noiseless distance, but after a while it fades from view, and it has no more than the wispy quality of a rumour. When you walk across Patrick's Bridge and the north side of the city lofts itself handsomely into being before you, it is hard to shake the sensation that you're at the centre of the universe.

The city is self-important but not in an egotistical way – it has such a solidity of atmosphere that, when you're there, it seems silly to consider that other places might have a similar heft or reality. Its atmosphere is very dense but it is made merely of these floating voices and shifting humours, of the fumes of the snarled teatime traffic, of the hoppy waft of the breweries – almost enough to drunken you on a clear bright winter's morning – of the dead-poultry perfume from the English Market, of the suggestions of a nearby sea, unseen but palpable, of the mildewed bedsits and the terraces that reek of three hundred days' rain. It is made of a starry night above St Fin Barre's Cathedral and a wet morning in the Glen as a white-arsed bunny tumbles into a hole in the hill.

But there are in fact other places in the world, and Cork's relationship with them is complicated. Its tendency with regards to Dublin, for example, is to studiously ignore it. To recognise it as an entity at all would be to grant that it might be considered as an alternative to Cork, even as a rival to it, and that would be ludicrous. When Cork people laughingly refer to the city as 'the real capital', the laughter is just a mask, or a defence mechanism – they are in fact utterly serious. Dublin is four times bigger, physically, but Cork people will insist that in terms of culture, food, pubs, natural beauty, hipness, setting, glamour, atmosphere, music and people, it is not just a little but markedly inferior.

6

If there is a great flaw that runs through the life of the city, it may be that it is so hopelessly attuned to class distinctions. There are some awful old snobs about the place. Read from almost any of the literature of Cork and this will quickly become apparent – beneath the surface of every sentence of a Frank O'Connor short story, the characters are being very precisely placed, socially, and to a near-neurotic degree. It's this that he springs almost all of his comedy from.

7

Cork is so careful with its money because there was ever only so much of it to go around, and it was kept in few enough hands. The merchant princes who have always run the city are perched still at a lofty remove above it. There is a certain Cork face – prosperous, pink, jowly and male – that has smiled over deals made in the vicinity of the South Mall for centuries. They bought and sold the place. They treated Dublin with disdain – trade ideally was with the Continent, and Cork was the most northern city of the Mediterranean. These princes still reign, though nowadays they retire when they're about fifty-two. They journey down the hills from their splendid Victorian terraces and have morning coffee with each other at the Imperial Hotel on the South Mall. I often stay there myself and I love to eavesdrop in the cafe around 11 a.m. They compliment the quality of the scones – where would you get *finer*? The sentence inflects at its end to a high-pitched lilt – all middle-class Corkmen have a natural campness. They talk of daughters in New York and boats in Kinsale. Their voices are running velvet, their eyes soft with nostalgia. They talk of the glory days on the Mall. They talk of it as a world within a world.

In many ways, Cork has always operated as a kind of city state, related but not quite attached to the rest of Ireland. In the early part of the twentieth century it had a share of industry unusual for an Irish city – it was more like a north of England city than an Irish one. And always there was an entrepreneurial streak. Sure didn't Henry Ford come from the *place*? (Italics for rising lilt.)

8

The Ford plant closed in the 1980s, and the city went into a steep decline. When I arrived, in 1992, it was noticeably on its uppers. This did the place no harm at all. It transformed it into a city ideal for creatives. The pubs were nearly full in daylight. There were very cheap pints being served. The Liberty on North Main Street (may it rest in peace) sold flagons of Linden Village cider over the bar. The Pot Black pool hall on Washington Street was a finishing school for young cannabis salesmen of unusual promise. The Frank and Walters were on *Top of the Pops*. The city remained utterly class-driven, except at Sir Henry's nightclub, on South Main Street, where all castes mingled in a cloud of Ecstasy and house music – the joke, among the posher student types at Henry's, was that you'd only realise who you'd been hugging when the lights went on at twenty past two, after the last song had been played (always 'Unfinished Sympathy' by Massive Attack). Some overheard dialogue, actual, recalled from the gents' toilet at Sir Henry's, between two young Corkmen, relating to their Ecstasy intake, some time around 1993:

CORKMAN 1: How many you on, boy?
CORKMAN 2: Six. And I have one at home for comin' down.

I was at this time the nightclub correspondent for a listings magazine in the city called the *Razz*. It was about as strenuous an assignment as I was capable of. In winter we used to go to parties all night and get up at half past six the following evening and eat rasher sandwiches. In the winter you wouldn't see daylight for months on end; you might just be up early enough of a January Saturday to get a bit of marshy grey twilight into you. It was a magical place.

Our flats were heated by turf briquettes and the glow of our fags. You could quickly lose track of your sense of ambition. All the same there was a healthy DIY ethic – people organised club nights, gigs, pirate-radio stations, theatre shows, art exhibitions, comedy nights, cabarets. When nobody has any money, everybody is as well off as everybody else. Most of the time nobody got paid. The normal escape hatch, when the city's tight perimeters seemed to close in, led always to London, not to Dublin – Dublin we ignored. I was going to do for South Main Street what Don DeLillo had done for the second half of the twentieth century in America – all I needed was a running start at it. There were pockets of evident melancholy as you walked the city in the middle of the night. The 'walk of shame' was at 4 a.m. to the Esso station on the Western Road to buy king-size Rizla. There was a huge inflatable tiger tied to the Esso station roof and people were always climbing up there and trying to cut him loose. A woman who wore a white cowboy suit used to stand in the middle of Washington Street and direct the traffic; she wore white cowboy boots, too, with gold sequins. You could see by people's eyes when the place was getting too much for them – there was a kind of smothered glaze that settled in, usually around February time. The city was given, as all small cities are, to cliques, and it was a place of ever-shifting allegiances. It was a beautiful city when it was empty in the middle of the night. After the last fights had blown themselves out by the cab ranks. When all to be heard was the beeping of the crossing lights for the blind on Washington Street. Or maybe the stray bark of a dog floating down from a north-side estate somewhere. Lovely then.

9

On the North Mall, I lived at number 23, and my landlady was fabulous, a woman named Helen Helen (Helen is an old Cork city surname). She was very kind, very old and very chatty, and she would tell me labyrinthine stories and ferocious gossip from around the town; often the stories would involve senior members of the

Garda Síochána whom she knew to be having affairs. If the walls of the Bridewell station could have talked at all. Helen Helen had the full suss on the city of Cork, in both its amorous and business affairs. I used to call upstairs to her to pay the rent and I'd end up there for hours, drinking tea and jawing the fat. She had watched the city for decades from her eyrie on the top floor of number 23. It was a very nice perch. The Lee eased itself past outside – no rush on – and we were right by the South Gate Bridge and so by the original spine of the city. The city was built up first between the two Gate bridges, along North Main Street and South Main Street. All sorts of ghosts and shades move there still, unseen and unceasing. Helen Helen pointed out the changes that were soon to come. They were knocking the old quay buildings across the river and putting up a cineplex and apartments. It will be unbelievable, she said, eagerly. She was delighted that the horrible old stone buildings were coming down – miserable damp places, she said, and not worth a spit. She died not long after this. The cranes and wrecking balls moved in across the water and the Gate cineplex went up and quickly another quarter of the old city had been taken apart.

10

B ut this is a city ever-memorious for its lost selves, and it has an atmosphere that conjures sentences. Time is never entirely fixed on these streets. There were the nights on Half Moon Street when the patrons would tumble from the Opera House and make for the Alaska Bar, singing as they went the songs that were popular then: 'Miss Me When the Twilight's Blue' or 'By the Light of the Silvery Moon'. The child John Whelan – later to reform himself as the writer Seán Ó Faoláin – would listen to them from the attic room of his home, a lodging house for touring hams and fourth-rate tenors and stage magicians, and it was a new century then, the twentieth, with horse dung and hay still ripe on the street's air, and everywhere the stench of fowl and coal smoke, and a rhythmic clanging all day and all night from the cooperage down the street. It was a city of wine vats and cobbled yards, and storied characters like Bob Helen and Ebenezer Bogan, and people still spoke of the gang fights that had raged between the Molly Malones and the All-For-Irelands. It was a city of hot, verminous slums and romance by dusk-light along the quays, the girls using their long black shawls to wrap their lovers tightly against them – on the Coal Quay the girls wore purple stockings and caps with golden tassels, the bright colours a rebellion against the city's natural hues, which Ó Faoláin caught so perfectly as 'the raingod's green, dark as passion, and this pallid immensity of sky'. It was a dark, damp valley, a miasma, but also it had steel at its heart, and sometimes enough to gleam.

11

A t some point I started working shifts for the local daily paper, the *Examiner*, and for its sister, the *Evening Echo*. I'd walk from the North Mall down the river and cut across Half Moon Street to the newspaper offices on Academy Street. This was half past six in the morning, and often I would be up late rather than up early. My first job was to phone every Garda station in Cork city and county and ask them if they had anything from overnight: 'Anything at all, lads?' There could be fourteen dead after a riot in Midleton but they wouldn't tell you unless you rang and asked them. It was very useful to get a look at the inner workings of a small city. In terms of fiction, the best research is the research you don't know you're doing at the time.

It was a proper old newspaper office, with a printworks out the back, a fine cuttings library, and it resounded all morning, as newspaper offices should, with the constant hacking of smokers' coughs. From the library, you could see out onto the main drag of Patrick Street, and I remember watching in awe what was in essence an early premonition of Celtic Tigerism. It was the run-up to the Christmas of 1999, the economy of both the city and the country at large had rebounded from a long recession, and everything was starting to thrum. The shopping on Patrick Street had taken on a fever-heated charge, almost a nastiness. It seemed as if people were scrawbing each other's eyes out to get into the stores. There was a monstrous quality to it. I don't think this is with the benefit of hindsight – I believe that even at the time it was clear that the city was coming up against the greatest threat yet to its independent spirit and ethos: the animalistic surge of twenty-first-century consumerism. Inside ten years, the *Examiner* had sold its beautiful old deco-fronted building on Academy Street to developers and moved down to the docks. The building is now an H&M.

12

The Well Inn, on the North Mall, was a pub where people would go when they were having secret flings. It was just far enough from the prying eyes of the city centre to be discreet. You reached it down a covered sideway that indisputably reeked of a medieval time, but that's neither here nor there. The Well was full of hidden nooks and crannies, and you could get a late drink, too – I believe that I was once pulled a pint there at half five in the morning. When I was living down the street, at number 23, I'd often go and drink quietly and watch the whispering huddles, and I'd make notes for short stories. I was going to do for hot-faced adulterers in Cork what Flannery O'Connor had done for wooden-leg-stealing Bible salesmen in Georgia. At this stage, my fiction writing was typically done at around 4 a.m. and at that hour the sentences would have the certain burnish of genius, were made of a moon-shot prose, were so vivid, glamorous and alive. Then the sober light of morning would creep in across the harbour. But the Well Inn certainly had the waft of 'material' in its air, and I was by now gathering material in a methodical way. I was training my ear. I was listening in. The city cried out to be fictionalised. There seemed to me to be far too little of it in print. The glorious language of its working-class estates had never yet put in an appearance in Irish literature, so called. (I was very cheesed off with Irish literature.) Characters seemingly ideal for fiction seemed to lurch into view all the time, from left and from right. There is a heightened theatrical quality to faces in Cork that's hard to describe – the faces can seem almost overdone, like in a David Lynch film, or like stone gargoyles from the Middle Ages. The gestures also can lean towards the overwrought. One night at the Well Inn a man of middle age, expensively dressed and with a face on him like a slow-roasted artichoke, stopped as he walked across the lounge, got down on one knee, wept aloud for about twenty seconds, stubbed a fag out viciously on his forehead, and then got up and walked out the door as if nothing had happened, his forehead marked as if it was Ash Wednesday. You couldn't put this in a short story – I know because I've been trying for years. You couldn't make it up.

13

I would spend hours trying to describe the place. 4 a.m. An empty flat. An electric typewriter (would you believe), a box of fags, and all the usual rookie mistakes – trying to describe something that had happened last week, or last month, or last year, without allowing the soak of time, and perspective, into the process. The flat I'm thinking of now was on Adelaide Street. I'd give up on the latest masterpiece, and I'd open the window back wide and sit on the sill and look out to the sleeping city and roll a spliff. I'd put on a record, low – usually dub reggae. The Cork accent can, to a suggestible ear, seem to have an almost Jamaican quality, and it was one of the better summers, maybe 1998, and the empty city streets by night seemed positively sultry, and I thought if you cut the place off from the rest of the island and let it float south, it might find at last its true coordinates, and its rightful place under the sun.

It often takes years to describe in fiction the places that you come from and that were formative for you. I was gone out of Cork nine years before I started to get it, in any way, on the page. When I'd used the city in short stories, the material, I felt, had always lurched into sentimentality. When I allowed it to creep in disguised, when I used it to give textures to a fantastical novel, *City of Bohane*, about a lawless Irish city in 2053, some of the proper notes started to come in, and I started to get the voices right.

14

You couldn't buy Italian sofas on McCurtain Street in my day. You could get a clatter outside the Uptown Grill at half two in the morning. But gentrification has made its soft-shoed shuffle along the north-side thoroughfare over the last decade or so. The effect is unmissable – there is a certain spruced-up quality where once there was scruffiness; the cafes and the stores are fancier; the people even seem a bit cleaner, a bit more groomed. The shoes are better. Something is missing, and something new has arrived.

Cork is an extremely liveable city and the secret appears to be out. It's much more multicultural now than it was – a process that began in the mid- to late 1990s has taken the mono-ethnic look off the place. It still seems at a slant to the rest of the island. I think it is at a delicate moment in its history, when it must decide what it needs to be. I hope that its future is as a creative place, that it accepts its true fate is to be a city of artists. Everything is in place to make this happen. The rents aren't bad; the coffee is good; the beer is excellent. The weather is given to violent mood swings but this is not unhelpful for those of creative temperaments. The city will thrive economically if it gives itself over fully to this happy fate – everything is in place, it just needs to be allowed to happen.

15

The best I ever saw it was through the eyes of an intense hangover. Christmas week, 1998. I'd been out very late but woke early, dehydrated, with a headache and a racing brain. All I could think to do was to walk it off. For once the raingod had relented – the morning was clear, blue-skied and very cold. I crossed the North Gate Bridge and went along the North Mall and climbed the Sunday's Well Road. As it snaked around towards the Western Road I was at an elevation above the city and above its valley and everything gleamed. I crossed the Shakey Bridge over the river into Fitzgerald's Park. A friend told me once the emotional high point of his life was the time he got a handjob on the Shakey Bridge. The park too was glittering – the frost had not yet thawed. I went up through the college grounds and back down Barrack Street – the scene of some of the most intense hallucinations of my life: I thought I was a traffic light – and onto the eternal roll of South Main Street, across Washington Street, onto North Main Street, and home. I was sick as a pig still but happy out. The city had never looked finer or felt luckier. ∎

HERE WE ARE

Lucy Caldwell

The summer is a washout. Every day the heavens open and the rain comes down; not the usual summer showers with their skittish, shivering drops but heavy, dull, persistent rain; true dreich days. The sky is low and grey and the ground is waterlogged, the air cold and damp, blustery.

We don't care. It is the best summer of our lives.

We go to Cutters Wharf in the evenings because nobody we know goes there. It's an older crowd, suits and secretaries, some students from Queen's. Usually we sit inside but one evening when the clouds lift and the rain ceases we take our drinks out onto the terrace. The riverfront benches and tables are damp and cold but we put plastic bags down and sit on those. It isn't warm but there is the feeling of sitting under the full sky, that pale high light of a Northern evening, and there is the salt freshness of the breeze coming up the Lagan from the lough.

After we leave Cutters Wharf that night we walk. We walk along the Lagan and through the Holylands: Palestine Street, Jerusalem Street, Damascus Street, Cairo Street. We cross the river and walk the whole sweep of the Ormeau Embankment. The tide is turning and a two-person canoe is skimming downriver, slate grey and quicksilver.

When we reach the point where the road curves away from the

river, the pale evening light still lingers so we keep walking, across the Ravenhill Road, down Toronto Street and London Street and the London Road, Willowfield Drive and across the Woodstock Road and on, further and further east until we are in Van Morrison territory, Hyndford Street and Abetta Parade, Grand Parade, the North Road, Orangefield.

There are times in your life, or maybe just the one time, when you find yourself in the right place, the only place you could possibly be, and with the only person.

She feels it, too. She turns to me. 'These streets are ours,' she says. 'Yes,' I say. 'Yes, they are,' and they were. The whole city was.

She was a celebrity in our school, in the way that some girls are. She was the star musician and always played solos at school concerts and prize days and when a minor royal came to open the new sports hall. One year in the talent contest she played the saxophone while another girl sang 'Misty'. They didn't win – some sixth-formers who'd choreographed their own version of 'Vogue' got more votes – but they were the act you remembered. She wore a white suit and sunglasses, but it wasn't that: it was the way she bent over her instrument and swayed, as if it was the most private moment in the world.

It was a few weeks later that her mother was killed. She was out jogging when a carful of teenage joyriders lost control and careened up onto the kerb. They didn't stop: if they had stopped, or at least stopped long enough to ring an ambulance, she might have survived. As it was, she died of massive internal haemorrhaging on a leafy street in Cherryvalley, less than a hundred metres from her home. Her husband was a local councillor and so it made the headlines: the petite blonde jogger and the teenage delinquents.

Her entire class went to the funeral, and the older members of the orchestra, too. I was only a second year and had never even spoken to her, so I just signed the card that went round. She didn't come to practice for several weeks and there were rumours that she had given up music for good. You'd look for her in the corridors, her face pale and thin with violet bruises under the eyes. Then one day she was there again, sitting in her usual place, assembling her clarinet, and if the teacher was surprised or pleased to see her he didn't let on, and none of the rest of us did, either.

She smiled at me sometimes in orchestra practice but I knew she didn't know who I was. I was two years below, for a start, and she had no way of knowing my name because the music teacher called all three of us flutes, Flutes. She smiled because he would make silly mistakes, telling us to go from the wrong place or getting the tempo wrong, and there'd be exaggerated confusion in the screeching, bored, lumbering ranks while he flustered and pleaded and tried to marshal a new start. People were cruel to him, sometimes even to his face. She never was: she just smiled, and because of the way the music stands were laid out I happened to be in the direction of the smile.

I used to say her name to myself sometimes. Angie. Angela Beattie.

What else? She cut her own hair: at least, that's what people said, and it looked as if it could be true, slightly hacked-at, although the mussed-up style made it hard to tell. Her father was a born-again Christian – he belonged to a Baptist church that spent summers digging wells in Uganda or building schools in Sierra Leone – and when our school joined up with another in west Belfast to play a concert at St Anne's Cathedral, she wasn't allowed to take part because it was a Sunday, even though it would be in a church, even though it was for peace.

There was so little I knew about her then.

In the summer term of fourth year, everyone took up smoking, or pretended to. The school was strange and empty that time of year, the upper sixth and fifth form on study leave, the lower sixth promoted to prefects and enjoying their new privilege of leaving the grounds at lunchtime. It was ours to colonise. We linked arms and ducked behind the overgrown buddleia into the alley behind the sports hall, boasting that we needed a smoke so badly we didn't even care if anyone caught us.

The day they did, it was raining and so we weren't expecting it: but all of a sudden there they were, coming down the alleyway, one at each end. I was holding one of the half-smoked cigarettes and I froze, even as all the others were hissing at me to chuck it away.

The prefect walking towards me was Angie.

I could feel the flurry as those with cigarettes or a lighter scrambled to hide them and others tore open sticks of chewing gum or pulled scarves up around their faces, but only vaguely, as if it was all happening a very long way away.

Angie stopped a couple of metres away. My hand was trembling now.

'Oh my God,' I heard, and, 'What are you at?' and, 'Put it out, for fuck's sake.' But I couldn't seem to move.

Angie looked at me. The expression in her eyes was almost amused. Then, ignoring the nervous giggles and whispered bravado of the others, she took a step forward and reached out for the cigarette. Her fingers grazed mine as they took it from me. She held it for a moment, then let it fall to the ground, crushed it with her heel. She looked me in the eye the whole time. I felt heat surge to my face.

'You don't smoke,' she said, and then she said my name.

I felt the shock of it on my own lips. I hadn't known she knew it: knew who I was. She gazed at me for a moment longer in that steady, amused, half-ironic way. Then she said to the other prefect, 'Come on,' and the second girl shouldered past and they walked back the way Angie had come.

'It's not cool, girls,' she called, without turning round. 'You think it is, but it's not.'

There was silence until they'd turned the corner. Then it erupted: 'What the fuck?' and, 'Oh my God,' and, 'Do you think she's going to report us?' and, 'I am so dead if they do,' and, 'What is she like?' and then, 'Do you reckon she fancies you?'

It was the standard slag in our school. But out of nowhere I felt my whole body fizz: felt the words rush through me, through and to unexpected parts of me, the skin tightening under my fingernails and at the backs of my knees.

'Wise up,' I made my voice say, and I elbowed and jostled back. 'It's because of the music. My lungs will be wrecked if I carry on smoking, I actually should think about giving up,' and because we

were always talking about having to give up, the conversation turned
and that got me off the hook, at least for the moment.

For the rest of term I agonised over whether to stop hanging out
with the smokers at lunch or whether to keep doing it in case she
came back. In the end I compromised by going behind the sports
hall as usual, but not inhaling, so I could say with all honesty, if she
asked, that I didn't smoke any more. My days became centred on
those ten minutes at lunchtime when I might see her again. I would
feel it building in me in the last period before lunch, feel my heart
start to flutter and my palms become sweaty. But she didn't raid the
alleyway again. There was nowhere else I could count on seeing her:
orchestra practice had ceased in the last weeks of the summer term
– the assembly hall was used for examinations and there were too
many pupils on study leave, anyway – and the sixth-form wing, with
its common room and study hall, was out of bounds to fourth years.
I passed her in the corridor, once, but she was deep in conversation
with another girl and didn't notice me. On the last day of term I saw
her getting into a car with a group of others and accelerating down
the drive, and that was that.

The summer holidays that followed were long. My father, a
builder, had hurt his back a few months earlier and been unable
to work so money was tight: there wasn't even to be a weekend in
Donegal or a day trip to Ballycastle. The city, meanwhile, battened
down its hatches and I was forbidden to go into town; forbidden, in
fact, from going further than a couple of streets away from our house.
All my friends who lived nearby were away; I was too old to ride my
bike up and down the street like my younger sister.

'Why don't you practise your flute?' my mother would say as I
sloped endlessly about the kitchen. Normally I'd roll my eyes, but as
the days stretched on I found myself doing it. I didn't admit to myself
it was because of Angie Beattie, but as I practised I couldn't help
thinking of her. When you first learn the flute, you're told to imagine

you're kissing it. Now, every time I put my mouth to the lip plate I thought of her. I'd think of her mouth, the curve of it. I'd think of the times I'd watched her at the start of orchestra practice, how she'd wet the reed of her clarinet and screw it into place, test it, adjust it, curl and recurl her lips around the mouthpiece. I'd let my mind unfurl and soon I'd think other things, too, things that weren't quite thoughts but sensations, things I didn't dare think in words and that afterwards left me hot and breathless and almost ashamed.

I got good at the flute that summer. When school started up again the music teacher noticed. He kept me back after the auditions and found me some sheet music, asked me to learn it for the Christmas concert. Then he said he'd had a better idea and rummaged in his desk some more. A sonata for flute and piano, he said: we were short on duets. Angie Beattie could accompany me.

'She might not want to,' I said.

'Nonsense,' he said.

I don't remember much about the first few lunchtime practice sessions we had together. Each one, before it happened, seemed to loom, so inflated in my mind I almost couldn't bear it; then, when it was happening, it rushed by. At first I could barely meet Angie's eye: it was mortifying, the extent to which I'd thought about her, let myself daydream about her, and more. But the music was difficult – for me, at least, which made it hard work for her as my accompanist – and that meant there was no time to waste; we needed to get straight to work. After the first week I found I was able to put aside, at least when I was actually with her, the memory of the strange summer's fantasies. But sometimes, late at night, I'd be consumed for an instant with an ache that seemed too big for my body to contain.

One evening we stayed late practising after school and, completely out of the blue, she invited me back to her house for dinner. My heart started pounding as I tried to say a nonchalant yes; I'd imagined her house, the rooms she lived in, so many times; I'd imagined so often a scenario in which she might ask me back there. I phoned my mum from the payphone in the foyer and then we walked back together, down the sweep of the school's long drive, through the drifts of horse chestnut and sycamore leaves in the streets, swinging our instrument cases. There was mist in the air, and as we turned off the main road, the taste of woodsmoke from a bonfire in a nearby garden. The Cherryvalley streets were wide and quiet, thick with dark foliage, lined with tall, spreading lime trees. It was a world away from my street, its neat brick terraces and toy squares of lawn. The gnomes and mini-waterfall in our neighbour's garden that I used to love and show off to school friends, before I realised they weren't something to be proud about. Cherryvalley seemed to belong to somewhere else entirely.

'It's nice around here,' I said.

She glanced at me. 'D'you think so?'

There was something in her expression I couldn't read and I remembered – of course, too late – that her mother had died here, maybe on this very street, or the one we just walked down. The streets felt not quiet, but ominous, then, the shifting shadows of the leaves, the plaited branches.

'I meant,' I said, flustered, 'the streets have such pretty names.'

She didn't reply and I tried to think of something else to say, something that would show I was sorry, that I understood. But of course I didn't understand, at all.

We walked on in silence. I wondered what had made her ask me back and if she was already regretting it.

The Beatties' house was draughty and dark. Angie walked through flipping on light switches and drawing the curtains. I thought of my house, the radio or the TV or often both on at the same time, my mum busy cooking, the cat always underfoot. Angie made me sit at the kitchen table, like a guest, while she hung my blazer in the cloakroom and made me a glass of lime cordial, then hurried about getting dinner ready. She turned on the oven and took chicken

Kievs from the freezer, lined a baking tray with tinfoil. Boiled the kettle to cook some potatoes, washed lettuce in a salad spinner and chopped it into ribbons. I had never, I realised, imagined how her home life actually worked. I felt shy of this Angie: felt the two years, and everything else, between us.

When Mr Beattie got back he looked nothing like the man you used to see shouting on TV or gazing down from lamp posts. He was tall and thin and washed-out-looking; his shoulders were stooped and his hair needed cutting. He shook my hand and I found myself blurting out, 'My dad used to vote for you.' It was a lie: my dad never bothered to vote and my mum, even though Dad teased her about it, only ever voted Women's Coalition. I felt Angie looking at me and I felt my neck and face burning.

'Good man,' Mr Beattie said. 'Every vote counts. These are historic times we're living through.'

'And history will judge us,' I heard myself say. I have no idea where it came from. The car radio, probably, the talk show Mum always had on and always turned off.

Mr Beattie blinked and Angie burst out laughing.

'Indeed,' he said. 'Indeed.'

'He likes you,' Angie said, when Mr Beattie had left the room. 'He really likes you.'

I wasn't sure what there had been to like, but before I could say anything, she said, 'If he talks about church, don't say you don't go.'

'OK,' I said. 'Why not?'

'Oh,' she said. 'It's just more trouble than it's worth.'

When everything was ready and the three of us sat down at the table, Mr Beattie bowed his head and clasped his hands and intoned a long grace. I looked at Angie halfway through but she had her head bowed and her eyes closed, too.

I took care to chime my 'Amen' in with theirs.

As we ate, Mr Beattie asked questions about school, about music. Often Angie would jump in with an answer before I had a chance and I couldn't work out if it was for my benefit or her father's. When he asked what church I went to, Angie said, 'She goes to St Mark's, don't you?'

'St Mark's Dundela,' Mr Beattie said.

'That's right,' Angie said.

'That's the one,' I said. St Mark's was where our school had its Christmas carol service, the only time of year my family ever set foot in a church, and only then because I was in the choir.

'Good, good,' Mr Beattie said, and I made myself hold his gaze. All that nonsense was just hocus-pocus, is what my dad liked saying. Once, when some Jehovah's Witnesses knocked on our front door and asked if he'd found Jesus, my dad clapped his forehead and said, 'I have indeed, down the back of the sofa, would you believe.' My sister and I had thought it was the funniest thing ever.

'St Mark's Dundela,' Mr Beattie said again. I started to panic then, trying to remember something, anything about it. But he didn't ask any more. 'C.S. Lewis's church,' was all he said, and I smiled and agreed.

The meal seemed to go on forever. The St Mark's lie had made me feel like a fraud: but it wasn't just that, the whole situation was putting me on edge. Angie was more nervous than I'd ever seen her: in fact, I couldn't think of a time when I had seen her nervous, not when she confronted the smokers, not even before a solo. I must be doing everything wrong, I thought. I had the horrible feeling, too, that Mr Beattie could see through me, or worse, could see into me, into some of the things I'd thought about his daughter.

For dessert there was a chocolate fudge cake, from Marks & Spencer, shiny and dense with masses of chocolate shavings on top.

'Dad has a sweet tooth, don't you, Dad?' Angie said. She cut him a slab of cake and they grinned at each other for a moment.

'We used to have chocolate cake for dinner sometimes, didn't we?' she said. 'Or cheesecake.'

'Strawberry cheesecake,' Mr Beattie said.

'We reckoned,' she said, turning to me, 'that because it had cheese in, it was actually quite nutritious.'

'A meal in a slice,' Mr Beattie said.

'Protein, fat, carbohydrate and fruit,' she said, turning back to him.

'A perfectly balanced plate,' he said, and they smiled that smile again, intimate, impenetrable.

When the meal was finally over, Mr Beattie said, 'Well, after all this talk of the duet, you must give me a concert.'

Without looking at me, Angie said, 'Another time, Dad, we're both played out today,' and I knew she was embarrassed of me. I felt tears boil up in my eyes and I stood up and said I needed the toilet. I took as long as I could in there, soaping and rinsing my hands several times over, drying each finger. I'd say I had homework, I decided. I'd say my mum didn't like me being out after dark. Both of these things were true.

When I told Angie that I had to go, she looked at me, then looked away. 'Oh,' she said. 'Right.'

Mr Beattie brought my blazer from the cloakroom and said he'd see me to the door.

'It's nice to see Angie bringing a friend back,' he said. 'I look forward to hearing this duet of yours one of these days.'

The whole way home I felt a strange, fierce sense of grief, as if I'd lost something; a possibility; something that wouldn't come again.

After that I avoided her, concert or no concert. I went with the smokers at lunch, half-daring her to come and find me, half-dreading it. Thursday and Friday passed without my seeing her. An awful weekend, then Monday and Tuesday, and on Tuesday afternoon I knew I had to skip orchestra practice. On Wednesday she came to the mobile where my class did French, in the middle of a lesson, and said to the teacher she needed to speak to me. She was a prefect and it was known that we were both musical; the teacher agreed without any questions. The shock and relief and shame of seeing her coursed through me and I had to hold onto the desk for a moment as I stood up. As I followed her out of the classroom and down the steps and around the side of the mobile I couldn't seem to breathe.

'How long are you planning on keeping this up?' she said.

'I don't know,' I said.

I could see her pulse jumping in the soft part of her neck. A horrible, treacherous part of me wanted to reach out and touch it.

'Angie,' I said, and from all of the things that were whirling in my head I tried to find the right one to say.

The trees and glossy pressing shrubs around us were thrumming with rain. All the blood in my body was thrumming.

'Look at me,' she said, and when I finally did, she leaned in and kissed me. It was brief, only barely a kiss, her lips just grazing mine. Then she stepped back and I took a step back, too, and stumbled against the roughcast side of the mobile. She put out a quick hand to steady me, then stopped.

'Oh God, am I wrong?' she said. 'I'm not wrong, am I?'

Two weeks later, in my house this time, a Saturday night, my parents at a dinner party, my sister at a sleepover. In the living room, in front of the electric fire, we unbuttoned each other's shirts and unhooked the clasps of each other's bras. Then our jeans and knickers: unzipping, wriggling, hopping out and off. We kept giggling: there we were gallivanting around in my parents' living room in nothing but our socks.

'Here we are,' she said, as we faced each other, and my whole body rushed with goosebumps.

'Are you cold?' she said, but I wasn't: it wasn't that, at all.

Afterwards we pulled the cushions off the sofa and lay on the floor, side by side. After a while we did start to shiver, even with the electric fire turned up fully, but neither of us reached for our clothes, scattered all over like useless, preposterous skins.

'We're like selkies,' she said, 'like Rusalka, do you know the opera?' and she stood up and struck a pose and sang the first few lines of the aria, the water nymph's song to the moon, she told me later, and I jumped to my feet and applauded and we started giggling again, ridiculous bubbles of joy.

'Here we are,' she said again, and I said, 'Here we are,' and that became our saying, our shorthand. Here we are.

All love stories are the same story: the moment that, that moment when, the moment we.

We were *we* through Christmas, and into the spring. It was so easy: the music had been the reason, and now it was our excuse. We used one of the practice rooms each lunchtime and sometimes after school, and no one questioned it. Sometimes we'd play, or she'd play and I'd listen, or we'd both listen to music, and sometimes we'd just eat our sandwiches and talk. I'd go to hers after school, although I never quite felt at ease there, and I preferred it when we'd go for drives in her car, up the Craigantlet hills or along the coast to Holywood. I drifted from my friends, and she from hers, but the music practice hid everything.

And then we had the summer and we were freer than ever, completely free, and I lied blithely to my parents about where I was going and who with, using a rotating cast of old friends, and neither of them ever cottoned on, and I assumed it was the same for Mr Beattie, too.

I don't want to think about the rest of it: the evening he finally confronted us; walked right in on us. I don't want to give any room to the disgust or the revulsion. To the anger and the panic that followed, and the tears, our tears, our wild apologies, when we should have been defiant, because what was there, in truth, for us to be apologising for, and to whom did we owe any apology?

Both of us, tears streaming.

'I have to do it,' she keeps on saying. 'I'm all he's got. It won't change anything. But I have to do it.'

I don't want to think about any of that, either.

That winter, my English class studied Keats. I wrote a whole essay, six, seven sides, on the final stanza of 'The Eve of St Agnes'. *And they are gone: aye, ages long ago | These lovers fled away into the storm.* In the stanza before, the lovers are gliding like phantoms into the wide cold hall and the iron porch where the porter lies in a drunken stupor. His bloodhound wakes and shakes its flabby face but doesn't bark. The bolts slide open one by one, the chains stay silent and the key finally turns, then just as they think they've made it the door groans on its hinges. You think it's all over for them but then you read on and you realise they've slipped away, out of your hands, before your very eyes, a miracle, a magic trick, a wormhole to another place, another time, where no one can ever follow.

The teacher kept me after class. She didn't believe I'd written it, at least not alone. I opened my lever arch and showed her my notes. Page after page in my crabbed, self-conscious writing. Ending rights the focus, I'd written, does not leave us in too cosy a glow but reminds us of age/decay/coldness of religious characters. I left this part out: I finished my essay with the lovers escaping. We talked about the real ending, Keats's ending, and we talked about his drafts of the ending, some of which were printed in the footnotes of the cheap Wordsworth edition.

'You've really thought about this,' she said. 'You've really taken this to heart.'

I started to cry.

'Oh dear,' the teacher said, and she found me a tissue from a plastic pouch in her desk drawer, and she came round and sat on the front of her desk and asked if there was anything I wanted to talk about. I shook my head and held out my hand for my essay, and I wondered how much she knew, or guessed, my whole body liquid with shame.

I looked up Angela Beattie on the Internet just once, some months ago, on impulse, spurred by the Marriage Equality march in Belfast. It instantly felt too easy: too much. She'd never made it as a solo or even an orchestral musician but she was a music teacher – and she was married; she and her husband ran a small music school together in Ayrshire. There were pictures of them both on the website, taking group lessons, conducting ensembles, standing with students from the most recent woodwind summer school. She was still whippet-thin, no make-up, choppy hair. He looked younger than her: Doc Martens and skinny jeans, spiky hair, an earring. I clicked from one picture to the next. I don't know why I was so taken aback. I was engaged, after all. Engaged, happily engaged, and about to buy a flat. I just had never imagined it for her.

A memory came to me: one time in Ruby Tuesday's, or The Other Place, one of the studenty cafes across town in south Belfast where you could sit and eke out a mug of filter coffee for a whole evening. We'd said I love you by then: maybe for the first time, or maybe very recently; we were huge and important and giddy with it, with all of it, with *us*. I felt as if my blood was singing – that sparks were shooting from me – that everything I touched was glowing. I could have done anything in those weeks. I could have run marathons or swum the length of the Lagan or jumped from a trapeze and flown. And yet I was happy, happier than I thought it was possible to be, just sitting in a cafe, talking. We sat in that cafe and talked about everything and nothing, talked and talked, and we were us. I remember that; I couldn't get over that. The room and everything in it – the scuffed wooden booths, the chipped laminate tables, the oversized menus; the fat boys in Metallica T-shirts and Vans at the table beside us, the cluster of girls across the way still in their school uniforms, the waitress carrying a plate of profiteroles; the rain on the window, the yellow of the light – it seemed a stage set that had been waiting our whole lives for us and at last we were here.

The waitress at the table, splashing more coffee into our mugs: 'Anything else I can get for yous, girls?' and we say, 'No, thank you,' in unison, then burst out laughing, at nothing, at all of it.

For all the waitress knows, for all anyone knew, we're just two students, two friends, having a coffee.

'I want to tell her,' I say. 'I want to stand up and tell everyone.' And for a moment, it seemed as if it might just be that simple: that that was the secret.

'I don't want us to have to hide,' I went on. 'I want to tell everyone – my parents, your dad. Everyone. I want to stand in front of the City

Hall with a megaphone and shout it out to the whole of Belfast.'

Suddenly neither of us was laughing any more.

'I wish we could,' she said.

We were both quiet for a moment.

'When you were older,' I said, thinking aloud, 'you could team up with a male couple and the four of you could go out together and people would assume, assume correctly, you were on a double date. Only the couples wouldn't be what they thought.' I was pleased with the idea, but she still didn't smile.

'Hiding in plain sight,' she said.

'You could live together,' I went on, 'all in one big house, so your parents wouldn't get suspicious. If you had to, you could even marry.'

I started laughing again as I said it.

'No,' she said, and she was serious, more than serious; solemn. She reached out and touched one finger to my wrist and all of my blood leapt towards her again. 'We won't need to,' she said. 'By then we'll be free.'

It all flooded back to me and made me indescribably sad.

That night, I walked the streets of east Belfast again in my dreams. Waking, the dream seemed to linger far longer than a mere dream. These streets are ours. I was jittery all day, a restless, nauseous, over-caffeinated feeling. I could email her, I thought, through the website. I wouldn't bother with pleasantries or preliminaries, I'd just say, There we were. Do you remember? ∎

Out

'Out' we would call it: we are going 'out' –
and the word was a kind of optimistic vapour
hung over evenings, redolent of light,
smoke, 'the encounter with a stranger
in Urban Space'
                    or in Belfast, some friend's friend . . .

'Out' was the clenched drive racing to the end
of every frothy, feminine half-sentence:
a missile aimed at ending difference
like an arrow tensed and sprung – arced out of sight
with this drink's end, and this, and this and this
– as the lamps went out and a bouncer shouted OUT –
like a ball whacked out of bounds and lost in moonlight . . .

The opposite of simply sitting about
in your head, like an egg in eggshell. That was 'Out'.

MR SALARY

Sally Rooney

Nathan was waiting with his hands in his pockets beside the silver Christmas tree in the arrivals lounge at Dublin airport. The new terminal was bright and polished, with a lot of escalators. I had just brushed my teeth in the airport bathroom. My suitcase was ugly and I was trying to carry it with a degree of irony. When Nathan saw me he asked: What is that, a joke suitcase?

You look good, I said.

He lifted the case out of my hand. I hope people don't think this belongs to me now that I'm carrying it, he said. He was still wearing his work clothes, a very clean navy suit. Nobody would think the suitcase belonged to him, it was obvious. I was the one wearing black leggings with a hole in one knee, and I hadn't washed my hair since I left Boston.

You look unbelievably good, I said. You look better than last time I saw you even.

I thought I was in decline by now. Age-wise. You look OK, but you're young, so.

What are you doing, yoga or something?

I've been running, he said. The car's just out here.

Outside it was below zero and a thin rim of frost had formed on the corners of Nathan's windshield. The interior of his car smelled like air freshener and the brand of aftershave he liked to wear to 'events'. I didn't know what the aftershave was called but I knew what the bottle looked like. I saw it in drugstores sometimes and if I was having a bad day I let myself screw the cap off.

My hair feels physically unclean, I said. Not just unwashed but actively dirty.

Nathan closed the door and put the keys in the ignition. The dash lit up in soft Scandinavian colours.

You don't have any news you've been waiting to tell me in person, do you? he said.

Do people do that?

You don't have like a secret tattoo or anything?

I would have attached it as a JPEG, I said. Believe me.

He was reversing out of the parking space and onto the neat lit avenue leading to the exit. I pulled my feet up onto the passenger seat so that I could hug my knees against my chest uncomfortably.

Why? I said. Do you have news?

Yeah yeah, I have a girlfriend now.

I turned my head to face him extremely slowly, one degree after another, like I was a character in slow motion in a horror film.

What? I said.

Actually we're getting married. And she's pregnant.

Then I turned my face back to stare at the windshield. The red brake lights of the car in front surfaced through the ice like a memory.

OK, funny, I said. Your jokes are always very humorous.

I could have a girlfriend. Hypothetically.

But then what would we joke about together?

He glanced at me as the barrier went up for the car in front of us.

Is that the coat I bought you? he said.

Yes. I wear it to remind me that you're real.

Nathan rolled his window down and inserted a ticket into the machine. Through Nathan's window the night air was delicious and frosty. He looked over at me again after he rolled it up.

I'm so happy to see you I'm having trouble talking in my normal accent, he said.

That's OK. I was having a lot of fantasies about you on the plane.

I look forward to hearing them. Do you want to pick up some food on the way home?

I hadn't been planning to come back to Dublin for Christmas, but my father Frank was being treated for leukaemia at the time. My mother had died from complications after my birth and Frank had never remarried, so legally speaking he was my only real family. As I explained in my 'happy holidays' email to my new classmates in Boston, he was going to die now too.

Frank had problems with prescription drugs. During childhood I had frequently been left in the care of his friends, who gave me either no affection or else so much that I recoiled and scrunched up like a porcupine. We lived in the Midlands, and when I moved to Dublin for university Frank liked to call me up and talk to me about my late mother, whom he informed me was 'no saint'. Then he would ask if he could borrow some money. In my second year of college we ran out of savings and I could no longer pay rent, so my mother's family cast around for someone I could live with until my exams were over.

Nathan's older sister was married to an uncle of mine, that's how I ended up moving in with him. I was nineteen then. He was thirty-four and had a beautiful two-bedroom apartment where he lived alone with a granite-topped kitchen island. At the time he worked for a start-up that developed 'behavioural software', which had something to do with feelings and consumer responsiveness. Nathan told me he only had to make people feel things: making them buy things came later on in the process. At some point the company had been bought out by Google, and now they all made hilarious salaries and worked in a building with expensive hand dryers in the bathroom.

Nathan was very relaxed about me moving in with him; he didn't make it weird. He was clean, but not prudish, and a good cook. We developed interests in each other's lives. I took sides when factional disputes arose in his office and he bought me things I admired in shop windows. I was only supposed to stay until I finished my exams that summer, but I ended up living there for nearly three years. My college friends worshipped Nathan and couldn't understand why he spent so much money on me. I think I did understand, but I couldn't explain it. His own friends seemed to assume there was some kind of sordid arrangement involved, because when he left the room they made certain remarks toward me.

They think you're paying me for something, I told him.

That made Nathan laugh. I'm not really getting my money's worth, am I? he said. You don't even do your own fucking laundry.

At the weekend we watched *Twin Peaks* and smoked weed together in his living room, and when it got late he ordered in more food than either of us could possibly eat. One night he told me he could remember my christening. He said they served a cake with a little baby made out of icing on the top.

A cute baby, he told me.

Cuter than me? I said.

Yeah well, you weren't that cute.

It was Nathan who paid for my flight home from Boston that Christmas. All I had to do was ask.

The next morning after my shower I stood letting my hair drip onto the bath mat, checking visiting hours on my phone. Frank had been moved to the hospital in Dublin for inpatient treatment after contracting a secondary infection during chemotherapy. He had to get antibiotics on a drip. Gradually, as the steam heat in the bathroom dissipated, a fine veil of goosebumps rose up over my skin, and in the mirror my reflection clarified and thinned until I could see my own pores. On weekdays, visiting hours ran from 6 to 8 p.m.

Since Frank was diagnosed eight weeks previously, I had spent my free time amassing an encyclopaedic knowledge of chronic lymphocytic leukaemia. There was practically nothing left about it that I didn't know. I graduated way past the booklets they printed for sufferers and onto the hard medical texts, online discussion groups for oncologists, PDFs of recent peer-reviewed studies. I wasn't under the illusion that this made me a good daughter, or even that I was doing it out of concern for Frank. It was in my nature to absorb large volumes of information during times of distress, like I could master the distress through intellectual dominance. This is how I learned how unlikely it was that Frank would survive. He never would have told me himself.

Nathan took me Christmas shopping in the afternoon before the hospital visit. I buttoned up my coat and wore a large fur hat so as to appear mysterious through shop windows. My most recent boyfriend, whom I'd met at grad school in Boston, had called me 'frigid', but added that he 'didn't mean it in a sexual way'. Sexually I'm very warm and generous, I told my friends. It's just the other stuff where the frigidity comes through.

They laughed, but at what? It was my joke, so I couldn't ask them.

Nathan's physical closeness had a sedative effect on me, and as we moved from shop to shop, time skimmed past us like an ice skater. I had never had occasion to visit a cancer patient before. Nathan's mother had been treated for breast cancer sometime in the 1990s, but I was too young to remember that. She was healthy now and played a lot of golf. Whenever I saw her, she told me I was the apple of her son's eye, in those exact words. She had fastened on to this phrase, probably because it so lacked any sinister connotation. It would have been equally applicable to me if I had been Nathan's girlfriend or his daughter. I thought I could place myself pretty firmly on the girlfriend-to-daughter spectrum, but I had once overheard Nathan referring to me as his niece, a degree of removal I resented.

We went for lunch on Suffolk Street and put all our luxurious paper gift bags under the table. He let me order sparkling wine and the most expensive main course they had.

Would you grieve if I died? I asked him.

I can't hear a word you're saying. Chew your food.

I swallowed submissively. He watched me at first but then looked away.

Would it be a major bereavement for you if I died? I said.

The most major one I can think of, yeah.

Nobody else would grieve.

Lots of people would, he said. Don't you have classmates?

He was giving me his attention now so I took another bite of steak and swallowed it before continuing.

That's shock you're talking about, I said. I mean bereavement.

What about your ex-boyfriend that I hate?

Dennis? He would actually like it if I died.

OK, that's another discussion, said Nathan.

I'm talking full-scale grief. Most 24-year-olds would leave behind a lot of mourners, that's all I'm saying. With me it's just you.

He seemed to consider this while I worked on the steak.

I don't like these conversations where you ask me to imagine your death.

Why not?

How would you like it if I died?

I just want to know you love me, I said.

He moved some salad around his plate with his cutlery. He used cutlery like a real adult, not shooting glances at me to check if I was admiring his technique. I always shot glances at him.

Remember New Year's Eve two years ago? I said.

No.

It's OK. The Yuletide is a very romantic time.

He laughed at that. I was good at making him laugh when he didn't want to. Eat your food, Sukie, he said.

Can you drop me to the hospital at six? I asked.

Nathan looked at me then as I knew he would. We were predictable to each other, like two halves of the same brain. Outside the restaurant window it had started to sleet, and under the orange street lights the wet flakes looked like punctuation marks.

Sure, he said. Do you want me to come in with you?

No. He'll resent your presence anyway.

I didn't mean for his benefit. But that's all right.

For the last several years, in the grip of a severe addiction to prescription opiates, Frank's mental state had wandered in and out of what you might call coherence. Sometimes on the phone he was his old self: complaining about parking tickets, or calling Nathan sarcastic names like 'Mr Salary'. They hated each other and I mediated their mutual hatred in a way that made me feel successfully feminine. Other times, Frank was replaced by a different man, a blank and somehow innocent person who repeated things meaninglessly and left protracted silences which I had to try and fill. I preferred the first one, who at least had a sense of humour.

Before he was diagnosed with leukaemia, I had been toying with describing Frank as an 'abusive father' when the subject came up at campus parties. I felt some guilt about that now. He was unpredictable, but I didn't cower in terror of him, and his attempts at manipulation, though heavy, were never effective. I wasn't vulnerable to them. Emotionally, I saw myself as a smooth, hard little ball. He couldn't get purchase on me. I just rolled away.

During a phone call, Nathan had once suggested that the rolling was a coping strategy on my part. It was eleven at night in Boston when I called, meaning it was four in the morning in Dublin, but Nathan always picked up.

Do I roll away from you? I said.

No, he said. I don't think I exert the requisite pressure.

Oh, I don't know. Hey, are you in bed?

Right now? Sure. Where are you?

I was in bed too. Not for the first time during these phone calls, I slipped my hand between my legs and Nathan pretended not to notice. I like the sound of your voice, I told him. After several entirely silent seconds, he replied: Yes, I know you do.

For the whole time we lived together he had never had a girlfriend, but occasionally he came home late and I could hear him through my bedroom wall having sex with other women. If I happened to meet the woman the following morning, I would discreetly inspect her for any physical resemblance to myself. This way I found that everyone in some sense looks like everyone else. I wasn't jealous. In fact I looked forward to these incidents on his behalf, though it was never clear to me if he enjoyed them that much.

For the last few weeks now Nathan and I had been sending each other emails about my flight details, what our plans for Christmas were, whether I had been in touch with Frank. I sent messages detailing my research, quoting from academic papers or cancer foundation websites. *In chronic leukaemia, the cells can mature partly but not completely*, the website said. *These cells may look fairly normal, but they are not.*

When we arrived outside the hospital that night and Nathan went to park, I said: You go. I'll walk home. He looked at me, with his hands on the steering wheel in exactly the correct position, as if I was his driving examiner.

Go, I said. The walk will be good for me. I'm jet-lagged.

He drummed each of his fingers against the wheel.

OK. Just call me if it starts raining again, all right?

I got out of the car and he drove off without waving to me. My love for him felt so total and so annihilating that it was often impossible for me to see him clearly at all. If he left my line of sight for more than a few seconds, I couldn't even remember what his face looked like. I had read that infant animals formed attachments to inappropriate things sometimes, like falcons falling in love with their human breeders, or pandas with zookeepers, things like that. I once sent Nathan a list of articles about this phenomenon. Maybe I shouldn't have come to your christening, he replied.

Two years before, when I was twenty-two, we went to a family New Year's party together and came home very drunk in a taxi. I was still living with him then, finishing my undergraduate degree. Inside the door of his apartment, against the wall with the coat hooks, he kissed me. I felt feverish and stupid, like a thirsty person with too much water suddenly pouring into their mouth. Then he said in my ear: We really shouldn't do this. He was thirty-eight. That was it, he went to bed. We never kissed again. He even shrugged it off when I joked about it, the only time I could remember him being unkind to me. Did I do something? I said, after a few weeks. That made you want to stop, that time. My face was burning, I felt it. He winced. He didn't want to hurt me. He said no. It was over, that was it.

The hospital had a revolving door and smelled of disinfectant. Lights reflected garishly on the linoleum and people chatted and smiled, as if standing in the lobby of a theatre or university rather than a building for the sick and dying. Trying to be brave, I thought. And then I thought: or after a while it just becomes life again. I followed the signs upstairs and asked the nurses where Frank Doherty's room was. You must be his daughter, the blonde nurse said. Sukie, is it? My name is Amanda. You can follow me.

Outside Frank's room, Amanda helped me secure a plastic apron around my waist and tie a papery medical mask behind my ears. She explained that this was for Frank's benefit and not mine. His immune system was vulnerable and mine was not. I disinfected my hands with a cold, astringent alcohol rub and then Amanda opened the door. Your daughter is here, she said. A small man was sitting on the bed with bandaged feet. He had no hair and his skull was round like a pink pool ball. His mouth looked sore. Oh, I said. Well, hello!

At first I didn't know if he recognised me, though when I said my name he repeated it several times. I sat down. I asked if his brothers and sisters had been to see him; he couldn't seem to remember. He moved his thumbs back and forth compulsively, first one way, then another. This seemed to absorb so much attention that I wasn't sure he was even listening to me. Boston's nice, I said. Very cold this time of year. The Charles was frozen over when I left. I felt like I was presenting a radio show about travel to an uninterested audience. His thumbs moved back and forth, then forth and back. Frank? I said. He mumbled something, and I thought: well, even cats recognise their own names.

How are you feeling? I said.

He didn't answer the question. There was a small TV set fixed high up on the wall.

Do you watch much TV during the day? I said.

I thought he wasn't going to answer that, and then from nowhere he said: News.

You watch the news? I said. That went nowhere.

You're like your mother, Frank said.

I stared at him. I felt my body begin to go cold, or perhaps hot. Something happened to the temperature of my body that didn't feel good.

What do you mean?

Oh, you know what kind of person you are.

Do I?

You've got it all under control, said Frank. You're a cool customer. We'll see how cool you are when you're left on your own, hmm? Very cool you might be then.

Frank seemed to be addressing these remarks to the peripheral venous catheter taped to the skin of his left arm. He picked at it with a morbid aimlessness as he spoke. I heard my own voice grow wavery like a bad choral performance.

Why would I be left on my own? I said.

He'll go off and get married.

It was clear that Frank didn't know who I was. Realising this, I relaxed somewhat and wiped at my eyes over the edge of the paper mask. I was crying a little. We may as well have been two strangers talking about whether it would snow or not.

Maybe I'll marry him, I said.

At this Frank laughed, a performance without any apparent context, but which gratified me anyway. I loved to be rewarded with laughter.

Not a hope. He'll find some young one.

Younger than me?

Well, you're getting on, aren't you?

Then I laughed. Frank gave his IV line an avuncular smile.

But you're a decent girl, he said. Whatever they might say.

With this enigmatic truce our conversation ended. I tried to talk to him further, but he appeared too tired to engage, or too bored.

I stayed for an hour, though the visiting period lasted two. When I said I was leaving, Frank appeared not to notice. I left the room, closed the door carefully, and finally removed my paper mask and plastic apron. I held down the lever on the dispenser of disinfectant fluid until my hands were wet. It was cold, it stung. I rubbed them dry and then left the hospital. It was raining outside but I didn't call Nathan. I walked just like I said I would, with my fur hat pulled down over my ears and my hands in my pockets.

As I approached Tara Street, I could see a little crowd had formed around the bridge and at the sides of the road. Their faces looked pink in the darkness and some of them were holding umbrellas, while above them Liberty Hall beamed down like a satellite. It was raining a weird, humid mist and a rescue boat was coming down the river with its lights on.

At first the crowd appeared vaguely wholesome, and I wondered if there was some kind of festive show happening, but then I saw what everybody was looking at: there was something floating in the river. I could see the slick cloth edge of it. It was the size of a human being. Nothing was wholesome or festive at all any more. The boat approached with its orange siren light revolving silently. I didn't know whether to leave. I thought I probably didn't want to see a dead human body lifted out of the Liffey by a rescue boat. But I stayed put. I was standing next to a young Asian couple, a good-looking woman in an elegant black coat and a man who was speaking on the phone. They seemed to me like nice people, people who had been drawn into the drama of it all not for tawdry reasons but out of compassion. I felt better about being there when I noticed them.

The man on the rescue boat placed a pole with a hook down into the water, feeling for the edge of the object. Then he began to pull. We fell silent; even the man on the phone fell silent. Wordlessly the cloth pulled away, up with the hook, empty. For a moment there was confusion: was the body being stripped of its clothing? And then it became clear. The cloth was the object. It was a sleeping bag floating on the surface of the river. The man went back to talking on the phone, and the woman in the coat started signalling something to him, something like: remember to ask what time. Everything was normal that quickly.

The rescue boat moved away and I stood with my elbows on the bridge, my blood-formation system working as usual, my cells maturing and dying at a normal rate. Nothing inside my body was trying to kill me. Death was, of course, the most ordinary thing that could happen, at some level I knew that. Still, I had stood there waiting to see the body in the river, ignoring the real living bodies all around me, as if death was more of a miracle than life was. I was a cold customer. It was too cold to think of things all the way through.

By the time I got back to the apartment the rain had soaked through my coat. In the hallway mirror my hat looked like a dirty water vole that might wake up at any second. I removed it along with my coat. Sukie? Nathan said from inside. I smoothed down my hair into an acceptable shape. How did it go? he said. I walked inside. He was sitting on the couch, holding the TV remote in his right hand. You're drowned, he said. Why didn't you call me?

I said nothing.

Was it bad? Nathan said.

I nodded. My face was cold, burning with cold, red like a traffic light. I went into my room and peeled off my wet clothes to hang them up. They were heavy, and held the shape of my body in their creases. I brushed my hair flat and put on my embroidered dressing gown so that I felt clean and composed. This is what human beings do with their lives, I thought. I took one hard disciplinary breath and then went back out to the living room.

Nathan was watching TV, but he hit the mute button when I came out. I got onto the couch beside him and closed my eyes while he reached over to touch my hair. We used to watch films together like that, and he would touch my hair in that exact way, distractedly. I found his distraction comforting. In a way I wanted to live inside it, as if it was a place of its own, where he would never notice I had entered. I thought of saying: I don't want to go back to Boston. I want to live here with you. But instead I said: Put the sound back on if you're watching it, I don't mind.

He hit the button again and the sound came back, tense string music and a female voice gasping. A murder, I thought. But when I opened my eyes it was a sex scene. She was on her hands and knees and the male character was behind her.

I like it like that, I said. From behind, I mean. That way I can pretend it's you.

Nathan coughed, he lifted his hand away from my hair. But after a second he said: Generally I just close my eyes. The sex scene was over now. They were in a courtroom instead. I felt my mouth watering.

Can we fuck? I said. But seriously.

Yeah, I knew you were going to say that.

It would make me feel a lot better.

Jesus Christ, said Nathan.

Then we lapsed into silence. The conversation waited for our return. I had calmed down, I could see that. Nathan touched my ankle and I developed a casual interest in the plot of the television drama.

It's not a good idea, Nathan said.

Why not? You're in love with me, aren't you?

Infamously.

It's one small favour, I said.

No. Paying for your flight home was a small favour. We're not going to argue about this. It's not a good idea.

In bed that night I asked him: When will we know if this was a bad idea or not? Should we already know? Because now it feels good.

No, now is too early, he said. I think when you get back to Boston we'll have more perspective.

I'm not going back to Boston, I didn't say. *These cells may look fairly normal, but they are not.* ∎

DISCOVER NEW TITLES
GREAT STORIES. UNIQUE PERSPECTIVES.

Unveiled - My Story
Shanon Jacobs

www.xlibrispublishing.co.uk

978-1-4931-9408-7 Hardback | £19.99
978-1-4931-9409-4 Paperback | £6.00
978-1-4931-9410-0 E-book | £1.99

Shanon Jacobs captures her life through poetry. She tells her story as a young woman struggling in life; how she managed from childhood to adulthood, scared and frightful at times, just to be brave at other times; how she conquered pain, the loss of a loved one, believing a higher power, and always having hope, ready to face another day.

I Believe
Garth Hodnett

www.xlibrispublishing.co.uk

978-1-4990-9605-7 Paperback | £13.99
978-1-4990-9604-0 E-book | £2.99

The Apostles' Creed is a simple statement of 12 beliefs – each central to Christianity. *I Believe*, translated by Garth Hodnett, is an important contribution to understanding the meaning of Christianity. Written in easy, but never superficial, language, this engaging book is for anyone who wants to gain a deeper appreciation and understanding of Christian thought.

A Product Of Insanity
Understanding Uniform Powers, Uniformity, Futuristic Military Dominancy 21st Century Thesis Ideological Warfare and More......
Sylvan Lightbourne

www.authorhouse.co.uk

978-1-4567-8389-1 Paperback | £7.74
978-1-4567-8469-0 E-book | £5.99

Product Of Insanity is literature for the 21st century minds. Minds that have transgressed from the 20th century into the 21st century with valour and bravery to earn the "beyond" with regards to how far the human mind can go, philosophically or metaphysically. This book will give you a sense of longing to understand free radical engineered thinkers.

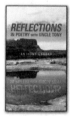

Reflections In Poetry With Uncle Tony
Anthony Gagbah

www.authorhouse.co.uk

978-1-4567-7831-6 Paperback | £6.99
978-1-4567-7832-3 E-book | £6.99

Reflections In Poetry With Uncle Tony captures the broad spectrum of human experience and attempts to engage the view points of readers in a manner that will provide a platform for dialogue in a poetic context. The author employs humour and lightheartedness to make all his writings relevant, relatable and emotionally accessible. Be inspired and invigorated today!

Chaffinch Charlie and Other Foibles
Jack Michael Weinblatt

www.authorhouse.co.uk

978-1-4208-9569-8 Paperback | £8.99

Chaffinch Charlie, a gangster retired to the Cost A lot, has a bar in which he runs girls for profit. But then his top girl runs off with a wealthy man and marries him, he gets upset. And now, he decides to take revenge on his previous employee, the lady that had run off to get married.

A Flower in a Box
Bradley Perera

www.authorhouse.co.uk

978-1-5049-8827-8 Paperback | £11.95
978-1-5049-8829-2 E-book | £2.99

A Flower in a Box is a collection of poems about the becoming of choice, delving deep into matters revolving around the interconnectedness of existence. Through pulses of rhythm and rhyme, it depicts the collective mindset shared between individuals. It artistically portrays the bond of people and how each one's thoughts and observations echo amongst each other.

Drama Lessons for Young Girls

Remember:
in a stage play every scene is driven by OBJECTIVES.
Every scene is driven by WHAT A CHARACTER WANTS.
DRAMA is created when objectives clash.

Here we see a young girl
cast as a young girl from the Acropolis,
moving elegantly forward,
and carrying an offering in her outstretched hand.
She is a figure in the act of worshipping.
She is holding out her hand –

but the outstretched hand is missing,
and where it was, is a stump of alabaster.
And her nose and her chin are missing,
and where they were, are two stumps of alabaster.
The lips are red, and the eyes are wide,
so she still looks like a pretty girl.

And her goddess is missing.
Athena has run off with the wolves.
They barked and howled and off she went.
Where has she gone?
What is it all meant to signify?

Remember:
in a stage play BAD DIALOGUE is expositional.
Characters OFTEN LIE.
They lie as a way of HIDING TRUTHS.

And hundreds of girls came bleeding to the door!
Their right hands outstretched!
But the grown-ups pulled the grille, and said:
you're naughty.
So the young girls,
cast as naughty young girls from the Acropolis,
left –
just with some things missing.
Their lips were red, and their eyes were wide,
so they still looked like pretty girls.

Remember this.

When the stakes grow in intensity,
it is known as BUILD.
DELAY is a dramatic device.
SUBTEXT is a character's DEEPEST SECRETS.

MY LAST DAY
AT SEVENTEEN

PORTRAITS FROM RUSSELL HEIGHTS

Doug DuBois

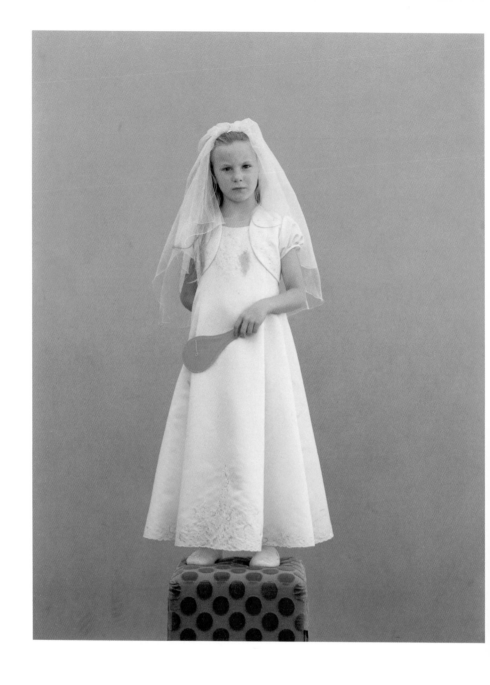

ARVON

Residential writing courses taught by leading authors

MARK HADDON

DAVID QUANTICK

MONA ARSHI

NADIFA MOHAMED

SUNJEEV SAHOTA

home to your imagination

"One of the most creative and enjoyable experiences I have ever had. I have never learnt so much in such a short time."

KEI MILLER

Supported using public funding by

ARTS COUNCIL ENGLAND

LOTTERY FUNDED

Grants available

arvon.org

THE VISITOR

Colin Barrett

The dog was some sort of overbred weedling with a ribcage fine-boned as a chicken's, a wizened rat's face and a goony, perpetually bloodshot stare that made Dev Hendrick want to punt the thing over the garden gate. Not that the creature ventured outdoors much, preferring the cosily cluttered terrain of the sitting room, where it spent its days mooching from cushioned niche to niche, secreting archipelagoes of vividly stinking piss stains on the chocolate corduroy couch and crooning with territorial rancour at anyone that was not Dev's mother. Now that she was dead, that meant everyone.

The dog was called Georgie, and the hate Dev nursed for it was deep and retaliatory. Georgie had come into the house five years ago, sized up the pair of incumbent primates, and set about ruthlessly supplanting Dev in The Mother's favour. Dev could not compete with the inhuman intensities of affection the dog embodied, its enthused yapping frenzies whenever The Mother reached for the meal bowl, its infant's mania for the tactile: whenever The Mother sat down, Georgie would instantly scrabble into her lap and remain ensconced there for hours if permitted, squirming sensuously as she ran her knuckles along its candyfloss pelt, its rat face a hideous mask of satiation, black lips peeled and yellow teeth showing. Dev could not compete. The Mother's cooking was mediocre, and he was too big a boy to sit up on her.

The one-up Dev had on the dog was that he still owned his own balls. Georgie had been neutered several years ago and was tormented since by recurrent seizures of phantom carnality. The closest Dev came to liking, or at least pitying, the creature, was when it mounted its proxy fuck toy – a stuffed Disney teddy bear with one eye missing, synthetic fur gone the smudged grey of a much used eraser – and quivered on its hind legs through a dusty travesty of coitus.

Georgie was doing just that, grimly pumping the nubbled posterior of the toy bear on the night the Ferdia brothers showed up with the boy. Dev was lying lengthways on the sofa with the TV on, laptop propped on his indrawn knees and his phone nestled in the hollow of his chest. He was drowsily watching the dog go at it, a mournful, fuddled expression in its clotted eyes. It was missing something, but it did not know what. Dev had been tolerating the urge to piss for nearly an hour, but was too lazy and comfortable to move. The phone started ringing and after three rings cut off. The Ferdias.

'Stay, shithead,' Dev said to Georgie.

He went into the hall, yawned, opened the front door. The sensor light mounted on the side of the house came on, illuminating three figures making their way up the drive. Gabe Ferdia at the front, Vincie at the back, a third person in a grey hoodie between them. The grey hoodie was watching his feet, picking his way among the stone chips littering the drive, the chips combed into mounds by the wheels of the cars that now infrequently dropped by. When they got to the door Dev saw that the hoodie was a teenage boy. The boy's head was shaven, his hairline an ashen chevron receding sharply at the temples. He had a wine-stain crease under one eye, a face like a baby girl's but for several skewed tines of silvery hair sprouting from his chin.

'He drunk?' Dev asked.

'Just a bit, yeah. Pulled him out of a house party,' Vincie said.

'Is he coming in?'

'He is, I'm afraid,' Vincie said. Vincie was the older and bigger of the Ferdia brothers. He touched the boy at the elbow and steered him through the door. Dev stood aside, admitted the three, then latched the door and followed them down the hall. In the kitchen, Vincie stood behind The Mother's old wicker chair and told the boy to sit. Georgie arrived from the sitting room, considered the three new presences and began barking shrilly at Gabe's shins.

'Stop, Georgie,' Dev said.

The dog startled. A chastened gurgle resonated in its throat.

'Do I know him?' Dev asked, nodding.

Vincie looked at the boy's crown.

'If you do it can't be helped. But do you?'

'No,' Dev said.

'That's all right. You don't know him. He's not in fact here, would be the best way to think of it,' Vincie said. He put a hand on the boy's neck. The boy's shoulders jinked fractionally from Vincie's touch. 'Though as it goes, Dev, we do need a room for him, just for a night. Two at the most, I'd say.'

'No way,' Dev said.

'I thought of you. Because this is important.'

'Uh-huh.'

Georgie was a fleck of incessant motion along the bottom of Dev's field of vision, an irritation, like a fragment of eyelash stuck on his retina he couldn't blink away.

'Sit, you little cunt,' Dev said.

The dog padded in a circle and promptly fainted on its back across the boy's shoes. The kid slid a foot out from under Georgie and rested the sole of his runner on the dog's palely haired belly.

'He likes you,' Dev said.

What Dev did was sit on drugs for the Mulrooney gang. The Ferdia brothers delivered, showed up every few months with bulky sports bags of stuff, sometimes much less. The stuff was sealed in sheets of waterproof plastic. Dev stowed each delivery somewhere dark and dry and forgot about it until the brothers returned. He had a couple of good places: a utility shed at the back of a field, the basement of the house if the sit was quick. Dev was a good sitter because he had no record and no public association with the county's criminal element. The Mother had died two years ago. A month after the funeral Dev quit his factory job. Since then he rarely ventured into town, or even out of the house. One night not too long after the funeral Vincie and Gabe appeared at the door. The Ferdias were cousins, but Dev had not seen them since school. They offered belated condolences on his mother. They said they heard about the job. They asked him if he wanted to make a bit of extra money to tide him over. The deliveries started a few nights later. This was the first time they had brought him a person.

'What's he called?' Dev was looking at Vincie.
        'Doon,' Vincie said.
'Moon?'
'Doon,' Vincie repeated. He came out from behind the boy, stood in front of him, studied the boy's knees.
'Stay put. Listen. Stay put. This is Dev. Do what Dev says. We'll be back in not too long.'
The boy's expression was sullen, densely remote.
Dev, Vincie and Gabe returned to the front door.
'Is he in trouble? Will he give me trouble?' Dev said.
'He's not in trouble,' Vincie said. 'He's just a spooked buck with a hangover coming on.'
'Who is he?'
'He's one of the Shandys.'
The Shandys. Dev had been to Dylan Shandy's place, once, back in school. He'd gone in with a couple of lads on a bag of weed. Shandy sold the weed, and they went to his house to collect it. It was a sunny day. Dev recalled a one-storey semi-d in the corner of an estate, a fenced front yard, the coils of a hose looped across the grass like an extravagant signature, a child's inflatable pool pruning as air seeped from it. Inside, a silent girl in jean shorts who was a crucial, inaccessible year or two older than Dev and his schoolmates, and Dylan Shandy himself, stocky and lordly, in flip-flops, with pale, fat,

hairy legs, the gear all over the kitchen table.

'I've been in Dylan Shandy's gaff,' Dev said. 'So this lad is something to Dylan Shandy?'

'Little fucking brother,' Gabe smiled.

'Why is he here?'

'The Shandy buck owes money to the Mulrooneys,' Vincie said. 'He owes money and is getting thick about it, suddenly thinks he's an expert' – Vincie here sighing, actually rolling his eyes heavenwards – 'on points of contract that don't, actually, exist.'

'Shandy's being a thick-headed fucker,' Gabe added.

Vincie put his hand up.

'The Mulrooneys need something over Shandy. When it gets like this, you need something over the other. All we did, me and Gabe, was walk into a house party tonight. And this fella?' Vincie nodded toward the kitchen. 'He was right there. Rank drunk in fact.'

'Head stuck in a freezer trying to cool off,' Gabe said, appalled.

'Credit that,' Vincie said.

'You took him out of a house?' Dev asked.

'You seen him. He's cut. He needs a place to flake out and soberise. We escorted him,' Gabe said. Gabe was thin and looked double his age. His teeth resembled lumps of tallow.

'This isn't good,' Dev said. 'He'll give me trouble.'

'He won't,' Vincie said. 'He'll sit and do as he's told. We wouldn't have got him this far if he wasn't going to do as he's told.'

'Compliant little sham,' Gabe said.

'If he tries to leave I'll let him,' Dev said. He was trying to sound stern, but the root of his throat was constricting, becoming hot and spongy, as Vincie went on with relentless evenness.

'He's just crashing here, Dev, sleeping off a heap of teenage cans. You should have seen the rest of them. We could have lifted any of the little fucks out of there. But we've all done it. When I was his age I could barely tie my shoelaces. That's the level of resourcefulness you're dealing with here. Feed him a stack of sausages in the morning, don't let him out of the house, he'll be happy out.'

Vincie flipped the latch and pushed open the door. The sensor light had timed out and clocked off. The night was summer mild. The Ferdia brothers stepped out.

'Will you call in the morning?' Dev asked.

'Of course,' Vincie said. He rolled his shoulders. Dev watched their backs, the duplicate hang of their gaits, as they crunched down the drive. They were about to disappear into the dark when the light came back on.

'What kind of dog is this?' It was in the boy's lap, coilingly orienting itself, trying to lick at his face. With each curling dart of Georgie's tongue the boy feinted his chin just out of reach.

'I don't know,' Dev said.

'How do you not know?' the boy grinned, suddenly alert now that the others were gone.

'It's my mother's. Ask her.'

'Your ma,' the boy said. He cuffed Georgie's ear. 'I will.'

'Yeah, well, you can't,' Dev grunted.

'Cos she's dead,' the boy said. He bent his head to the dog. 'Some mix of a Pomeranian and something else, I'd say. Dainty little showpiece. But these things get messed up. Poor lungs.' He gripped the dog under its scrawny forelegs, lifted it into the air with a veterinarian's dextrously brutish matter-of-factness, and pressed his ear against its elongating belly. 'Hear that. System's all gunged up.'

Dev shrugged, bewildered.

'Put it down.'

The boy guided Georgie back to his lap and eased his grip. The dog slithered down the boy's knees and scuttled a yard clear of him, retreating beneath a chair and from there eyeing the boy with a kind of grudging reverence.

'You hungry?'

'I haven't done anything,' the boy said.

'You hungry?'

'They took my phone.'

Dev pulled the fridge door. It resisted, then popped free, condiments chiming against each other in the door's shelf. 'If you don't want anything, that's fine, but there won't be anything else until morning.'

Dev removed a rib sandwich from a plastic container, plated it, and nuked it in the microwave for sixty seconds. The boy watched Dev as he watched the plate revolve in the treated glass of the machine's window. The microwave pinged.

'There.'

When Dev stepped close to the boy he saw that the injury to his eye had evolved, fraying threads of blood now strobing the eye's white like a raspberry ripple.

'Did they do that?'

The boy's jaw began to putter, his mouth shrinking to a stony ruck, his eyes crisping with tears. He stood up, sat down, jumped back up and screamed. Dev palmed the flat of the plate against the boy's chest and watched the circle of white delft crack cleanly in half. The rib sandwich flopped against Dev's forearm, hot. The boy's hands were on Dev's arms, fingers digging deep. Dev grabbed the boy's throat and shoulder and the split plate fell. The boy was pushing forward, as if trying to climb up over Dev's shoulders. Dev drove his thumb into the jumping braid of a tendon in the boy's neck, guddled a knee between the boy's thighs, and pushed in the direction of the wicker chair. Dev's muscles were spasming and he thought he was about to collapse when the boy gasped, moaned and went slack within Dev's grip. A wave of exhaustion washed over Dev as the boy wrenched back down into the chair. Dev stood back, his legs jumping and twitching in place.

He watched the boy smooth the thighs of his denim jeans, arrange the disordered neckline of his hoodie. The boy blinked emphatically several times, as if corroborating some inner calibration, then put his hands to his temples and pulled his head down onto his knees. He pressed the ends of his fingers against the back of his skull, so hard his knuckles began to whiten. Wet babyish noises escaped his lap. Dev cleared his throat, recleared it, swallowed a gob of sputum. His blood was spouting in its grooves. He felt dizzy and addled, warm in his core and vague at his extremities, as if he'd emerged from a long time in a steam room. He looked around. The plate had broken into further pieces on the floor. Georgie was already over the rib, heartily chowing down on the warm meat.

Dev's breath was short and rushed, the edges of incomprehensible words flitting from his mouth before he could snag them and speak. Finally, he found he could talk.

'If you don't. If you don't do that. Again. I won't tell.'

'I didn't do anything,' the boy groaned into his thighs.

'This isn't anything. This isn't anything,' Dev said and kicked the largest fragment of the broken plate across the kitchen floor.

He couldn't let the boy out of sight so made him come upstairs. The boy waited in the hall while Dev pulled bedding from the boiler closet. Into the boy's arms he piled folded sheets and a sleeveless pillow grainy with must. The pillow was torso-sized, its stuffing wadded into lumps, like muscle that had lost its definition. Dev balanced a rolled-up blanket on his shoulder with hairs that itched at his neck. Georgie was watching them from the top of the stairs, pacing imploringly back and forth on the final step and refusing to come closer.

In the kitchen, Dev punched the goitred pillow into an approximation of pillowyness and tossed it back at the boy. He wanted to keep the boy's hands occupied. The door to the basement was between the fridge and the door to the back garden. Dev opened the basement door, reached into the cool, raw dark for the light panel. The basement bulb was naked, stubbled with dust motes that singed as the bulb heated up. The basement floor was unpainted concrete, and looked as cold as lake water. There was a mattress on a metal-spring frame, a desk with an old, fat, dust-caked computer monitor and a hard drive the size of a suitcase on it, a hank of cables descending into an intestinally knotted heap under the desk, the prongs of the white plug heads glinting in the dim. Dev had spent much time here as a teenager. Other kids went out. He went under the floorboards.

'I'll stick the heating on for an hour. It'll warm up down here, but if you want to just get under the blankets with your gear on.'

Georgie brushed into the gap between the boy's legs, inspected the revealed depth.

'I should put him in here with you. Company,' Dev said.

'Don't do that,' the boy said.

'I'm kidding.'

'You put that dog in with me and I feel like I will murder the thing. I'll make it suffer.'

The boy did not look murderous, only, again, on the verge of tears. Dev was angered, not because of the threat, but because it was a convictionless lie.

'That's my mother's dog, you stupid little shit. No one gives a fuck about you, and that's the truth. What are you even doing here? No one cares. That's the truth.'

'I didn't do anything,' the boy said again.

Dev picked up the bedding and the blanket, steadied himself and flung them down the stairs. The sheets plumed in the cold dark air and snagged on the stair steps.

'Get in.'

Dev debated locking the door. He had to. He would set his phone alarm for 6 a.m. At dawn he would unlock the door, and if it ever came to it, would claim the door had never been locked at all. Believing he could undo anything he was about to do gave him the resolve to do those things. He locked the door. If he had not, he knew he would not sleep. He likely wouldn't anyway. There was the possibility the boy might try and smash his way out: there were implements, things down there he could try as a bludgeon. But Vincie was probably right. The boy claimed he had done nothing, but he was going along more than he should have. Even if his compliance was just a way of buying time, it was still compliance. Dev did not know the boy but he already hated him enough to see the night through.

He went back upstairs, to his own bedroom, and hefted down his mattress. He cleared a space on the kitchen floor, threw a blanket on it. He sank onto the raft of this makeshift bed and an appendicital jab in his side reminded him he still had not peed. To remain within sight of the kitchen, he went outside and a little way down into the back garden.

It felt good to piss outside, the night air around him. Georgie came out, face truffling in the grass, weaving back and forth like a dowsing wand. Dev could hear Georgie panting, imagined he could make out the racing dicker of the dog's minuscule heart. The arc of Dev's stream wavered and guttered out like a candle flame. He jounced in place to dry off, looked around.

'Georgie?'

The bottom of the lawn was too dark to make anything out, but Georgie, an inherently unintrepid creature, was surely still just there. It was only that Dev couldn't see. He listened. The garden ended in a rotting wooden fence. Beyond the fence was a mound of amputated vegetation, then crop fields. Dev listened for the dog, and out of the silence rose a minglement of remote, delicate and richly inhuman sounds; papery rustlings and scuttlings, tricklings and clicking secretions. He said the dog's name again and turned and started toward the house. Georgie appeared and had already gone in ahead by the time Dev got to the kitchen entrance. Inside, Dev moved past the basement door and without looking brushed a fingertip against the looped handle of the key protruding from the lock.

He retrieved his laptop from the couch and made a bowl of cornflakes. He ate them slowly as they turned to slime, desultorily surfing, opening tabs and multiplying links in an attempt to postpone looking at the basement door. Every time he imagined going over and turning the lock a heat flash startled along his neck. He held his breath at intervals, the better to listen into the depths of the house; but he heard nothing, only the ambient hum of the domestic electricals.

It felt to Dev like he was listening to the house listen to its own silence. Twitches, stray darts of voltage, coursed through the meat of his thighs. It was exhausting and agonising to not move.

He shut down his laptop, stood up, and turned off the kitchen light. He stood for a moment in this sudden, self-inflicted blindness, the darkness like a fresh contusion pulsing into the sockets of his eyes. It was like he had punched himself in the face. He groped his way to the mattress and sank onto it with the careful grogginess of a punched man. Georgie came over, panting in rapid, stinking darts, tongue flicking at Dev's hanging fingers. Dev shifted, opened out his arm and the dog scrambled up into his armpit.

'Settle, you cunt,' he whispered.

Dev had aligned the mattress with the basement door, had pushed back the chairs to permit himself an unobstructed view. He propped himself against the pillow. It was too dark to see anything.

Dev had recurring dreams about the house. In the dreams the house was this one, but its interior was changed, mutated. He would for example go upstairs and find that the landing extended deep beyond its regular dimensions. There would be an extra, unopenable door or supply closet built into the walls, or blank drywall where a window or door should have been. The turns in the hallways went the wrong way, left instead of right, or vice versa. Electrical cabling and wiring coming through broken plaster like ganglia. In the dreams Dev would wander these transformed, overgrown spaces but there was never anyone else there.

Georgie's dog breath thrummed against his ribs. Dev was awake again. He blinked. The dark had taken on grain and texture. He could see it, could see through it. For a relieved moment he thought he was looking at nothing, but there, in the dark, the basement door, the pale glowing length of it, began to appear. ∎

GREEN, MUD, GOLD

Sara Baume

Two cousins stand at the foot of a prodigious field.

Neither knows how far it goes because it rises up a slope, falls down the opposite side and disappears. The part they stand at is its lowest step, its shallow end, its bottom rung. To two sides, there is field, to one, there is road. To the other, there is the gable of their grandfather's bungalow, painted sun-glow and pebble-dashed, a fibreglass fawn peeping up from the lawn, a bilberry shrub, a picket gate.

The sky's yet filmed with daylight, even though it's late,
because it is midsummer.

Both cousins rent rooms in cities now, with flat-pack bedside tables, laptop computers, rat-king tangles of USB cables, but roomed here first, in the field belt. Of all fields in the belt, they should know this one: its steps, shallows and rungs, beginnings and ends; this is the one in which all their open-air games took place,
every type of hide and chase
every seek.

But Grandfather always told them to stay, to play on this side of the hill with the village below, where they could be seen through his field-facing window, and both cousins were the kind of little girls who did as they were told.

And now, they are girl-women: twenty-one, twenty-two; one dark, one fair. Their costumes are infinity bras and magic knickers, plumes of polyester hair. They stand swaying in rhythm with the crop, at the whim of the warm wind, drunk as wasps on jam; drowning in jar traps as weary bees fed their own strange honey back to them from squeegee bottles.

Fugitives from the reception of a family wedding, from a giant tent in their grandfather's garden, three different catering vehicles. They left during the closing phase, the makeshift disco, only noticing the slur in their voices, the slur in their gestures, when the waiters took their chairs away. They wanted to dance, but not there in front of grandparents, godparents, real parents, no chance, even though they are old enough, even though they've been much drunker, many times, on floors where their families couldn't see.
So they'd decided to dance, to slur, here instead.
Let's go up to the field, Fair said,
she whispered.

Field has metamorphosed over the years, from mud to beet to spud to meadow, to rape to oats, and then, once men in lab coats developed extraordinary pesticides so that men in mud-doused boots barely needed to rotate their tillage any more, it went from spring barley to winter wheat, to spring barley to winter wheat, to spring barley to winter wheat.

And how bored Field is now, stitched beneath the hardly varying view, doomed to exist for all time to come and having existed for all gone, though it has not always been a field, of course. Before, it was forest.

Before forest, ice.

Before ice, mainland.

Before mainland, sea.

And now two cousins stand at its flank, in its lee, and don't care about history. They care about eyelash curlers and fruit-flavoured condoms, about the eco-friendly confetti which adhered itself to their bronze-shimmer tan and dissolved, about whether or not people they don't even know think they're pretty.

This day, of the wedding, there was a callow sun at dawn, a shower during the interminable ceremony, a lily-livered rainbow and wet laurel for the photographs. There was a white car, a white dress, a white marquee, a white sky which made it hard to distinguish between car and dress and marquee. To Field, the wedding looked like an aggregation of fancy hats, of frills and feathers and fascinators nodding against the white. Like a triad of bridesmaids in puce and plum and periwinkle, five hundred LEDs a twinkle, a jumble of timber table legs protruding from beneath the white cloths. And suspended above: white wine, white fish, white bread, a champagne sorbet which arrived in a flute capped with a strawberry and was white too.

It was back then and there that Dark and Fair found their names embossed on white rectangles side by side,
and so, allied.

Fair wears a harvest-moon dress, oxblood lipstick and platform pumps with ballerina ribbons in ankle bows. Dark's dress is longer, its fabric printed with exotic flowers: frangipanis, orchids, little bells. The cousins chose the same dishes on the menu, neglected all the sprigs of rocket and lamb's leaf, divided the flesh of their hake pleat by pleat, as if only learning that fish are welded together in this fashion, like onions; as if searching for white-gold pin bones between the folds.

Then the tables were stripped and carried away; the crumbs and crumpled napkins swept up, the chairs stacked up, and everybody got up and started dancing in different styles to the same songs. The old tapped their new shoes and waltzed across the improvised floor, the young jiggled and jumped and bumped against one another, like lunatics in padded cells, groping for a door.

And Dark and Fair, stomachs sloshing with a vile soup of alcohol and hake, of white cake which turned out to be chocolate, found, the last free, full bottle of Sauvignon Blanc, and absconded, field-bound.

They stumbled across Grandfather's lawn, hopped over Grandfather's fawn, his shrub, and out on the road, they slowly ascended the incline, to the farmer's gateway, the brink of belt, the undulant skyline.

The barley is five foot, the cousins barely taller. Gold, ripe, ready, somehow both soft and sharp, both stirring and steady. The tyre tracks of the farmer's contraptions: tractor, sprayer, spreader, planter, run up and down, over and back, cross-hatching Field. The cousins set out along the first they meet, passing junctions as they traipse. The track is perfectly clear, as if it has been prepared for them: pruned, swept and steam-rolled in their honour; no weeds, no errant shoots, just clean dirt, supple such that their heels sink a fraction with each step, such that they stagger ever-so-slightly more than they already staggered across the dance floor, on the firm and flat. From sky level, this patch is scribbled with disordered lanes, but from eye level, Field is a choppy green-gold sea through which they are wading, the wedding fading, only the glow of its illuminations remaining visible through the dim, above the rising crop tide. And to its pastured side, as they approach, the grazing stock stop grazing, merge together and surge toward the cousins, come as close as they can to the tautly strung wire, ticking with volts, clucking its electric tongue in reproach, come so close they threaten to cheese-knife themselves, to keep coming in their seared slices.

Neither cousin knows where Field ends; neither cousin knows if Field ends.

So they allow themselves to be led, bearing on toward the horizon until Fair guesses they are halfway, breaks off from the path, throws her limbs and skin and dress down on the throng of stalks, and Dark follows.
And swallows,
still hunting, even though it's almost night, dipping the surface with beaks open wide, a clownish kind of flight, a hesitant pitch and glide, like shuttlecocks. The cousins lie still and feel their bodies moving even though they are not moving their bodies: blood percolating, pupils dilating, nerve endings sparking, until Fair is up again, this time her movements surer, swifter.

I'm making a crop circle! she cries, and starts to kick down shoots as if she can see a pattern in her mind, as if she's sketching a picture on the island's surface, a gift for passing aircraft: a curlicue, a doily, a spirograph. For a while, Fair pummels the barley and Dark listens to each stalk soft-scream as her cousin buckles it; lies lifeless as she listens, like a murdered thing, waiting to be buried. And a rift opens between them, Dark so impassive, Fair so intent. And Field sees, and Field feels, and Field recognises this chink, this breach, this rent.

The mud clenches, the felled stalks whimper and the standing ones crackle. The sky obscures, as if a cloud covering the sun, only there is no sun and the sky is all cloud, all covered. And Fair stops, checks, sees that the pattern in her mind has failed in front of her face.

Sees only ravage, ruin, a messily cleared space.

And so down she bellyflops again, reaches for the bottle, slugs, draws her knees up to her chest to hug, and it's only now, and suddenly, that the cousins understand how much more powerful than them the crop is, how much vaster than them the field is, how every root and shoot and leaf and grain is commanded by Field.

They lie,
bottle in-between, good wedding clothes freckled by some beige-coloured kind of chaff or seed, some leaked filaments of a weed, by a black bug coiled up like a tiny bead, another and another. They'd forgotten about insects; in their rented rooms there are no moths or beetles or flies, only an occasional house spider who tripped, slipped into the sink and trapped, starved, died.

They lie,
together, the cousins, remembering Roy Rover, Simon Says, Bulldog, Tip the Can, and Field eavesdrops and is never consummately silent, because even if the birds and bugs stop, the wind won't; because even if the birds and bugs and wind stop, the clay will continue to murmur, to purr.

They lie,
until Fair robs the emptying slug, pushes herself up and, realising they have been unlaced, kicks off her ballerina platforms, beats away from Dark and into the dark, shouting:
You're it! Start counting!

But Dark cannot count, she is too drunk, and so she only watches from the ground how the barley Fair had levelled does not stay slack but springs back, closes behind her like a trap. Dark can still hear running, shouting, but the sounds shrivel as the seconds lapse, until there's only the sound of Field: wind whipping shoots and purring clay, the burring of forgotten night flies.

And Dark lies,
as Fair left her, limp on the slain and trampled crop, listening to the sounds stop, watching the obscured sky deepen. And even though she knows that deepened sky means caving time, she does not get up. She lies prone, alone; still but doesn't feel still. She feels instead as if there is a field inside her, swishing her platelets, pin-prickling her tissues. She shuts her eyes and pictures ears growing out through her ears, her spine turning to wood, pictures herself as a girl-woman scarecrow, arms opened wide,
and nailed to two posts in the centre of a great green, mud and gold expanse,
crucified.

What did we use to tip here? Dark asks no one, aloud. Never actual cans, not once. Gutter pipes, swing sets, flowerpots, in other places, but she can't remember what it was here, in Field, where nothing stands up or is fixed down, where there are no landmarks at all, nothing taller than the stalks, nothing not made of plant.

She wants to get up, but thinks she can't,
she tries, trips, retches. Now the birds have been replaced by bats, the gnats by midges. Dark digs her heels into the pliant earth, looks around. But she can see no field-furniture to tear toward, to touch, to tap. No lights in the distance, no lights in the air, no Fair. She can see nothing but fretful vegetation and caliginous universe. How can it be that Field is suddenly so tremendous? Dark tries to think, can't think.

How can the bungalow be so far away; how can the lights of the wedding have gone out all in sync?
She shouts her cousin's name, her voice begins to break, to shatter, the barley shakes, bats scatter, and Field steals Dark's cry, sculpts it into a squeak, a scoff, a sigh.

And in every limitless direction, there are a billion trillion tiny ears, but no cruel-meaning creatures make their home here on this harmless land mass of perpetual murk, this island designed by glaciers for the benefit of trees, where the ground is ever hilly, the earth ever unyielding. No snakes in the towering grass, no sharks in the green-gold sea, no wolves in the stalk forest; these ears belong to the barley, and soon they'll be chopped and stripped, plastic-wrapped and packed.

Dark wrests her feet free, tugs them up as if her shoes are patent leather leeches spat from the soil and suctioned to her soles. Barefoot, she runs, the tyre path smooth and cold, her long, light, bright chiffon snagging, shredding, and the fronds which had caressed, now lacerating, leaving exotic-flower streamers, frangipani, orchid, little bell, in her wake.

Midsummer. Night. Dark in the dark field.

And, just maybe, a wolf, a shark, a snake.

Running, slipping, tripping, ripping, Dark raises her hands above the surface of the track, to flap for help, and Field sends its rooted shoots reaching up too, growing as she watches, waving back.

How can it be, she asks herself, aloud, that these shoots sewn, rooted, sealed into the mud a billion, trillion times can be chasing me; how can Field go on eternally?

And to the aircraft which do not pass, Field might look like a monstrous piece of toast, a scrubbing brush coated with pollen, a close-shaved animal pelt. From the air, there are no bounds; there is no belt,
every where and thing is Field.

And Dark bellows her cousin's name, again, the same, and hears, this time, a panicked squawk, and wants to believe it came from Fair, but knows it can't be so, and lo, the crop discharges a pheasant, a squabbling emerald-brown ball, startling Dark so that she falls, and spreads her fingers to break the impact, covers her head as if the bird might descend again, to attack. For a moment, commotion, but now, a great lull. Dark's cheek pressed against the path as if she might listen her way to her cousin through its smooth mud arteries, smooth mud nerves and smooth mud veins.

Abruptly, Dark realises, that Fair is just lying down somewhere, along one of these crop lanes,
like she is, only passed out, slumbering, drunk-dreaming. And Field turns its ears down toward fallen Dark, reminding her that they are gold, that gold means ripe, that ripe means a combine harvester, an artillery of spinning blades sweeping,
a screech for every sundered shoot,
a girl-woman sleeping.

Up Dark leaps, again, sprints, howls.

I should have been a forest, Field thinks; she should be beating her way through bracken, branches thwacking, grappling blind, drunk, from trunk to trunk, pursued by glint-toothed predators, stags and stoats,
weasels and owls;
That would have been more amusing, Field thinks.

On Dark dashes, receiving a thousand barley lashes. But finally she stops, pushes her body onto the balls of her toes in order to see over the top of the crop. And what Dark sees, way way off, is a dark dot skimming the surface. Not a bird, too late. Not a bat, too round and heavy and low. But what can only be a head, a head not wholly skimming but bouncing slightly, not lightly, hesitantly, like a shuttlecock, but solidly, certainly, as if the body beneath the head, the feet beneath the body, are bounding. She is so weary now, her skull pounding, all her slackened muscles tight. Her eyes are filled with particles of grating gold; she blinks, claws at her sockets, begins to cry as if crying were a practical measure, a way to clear her sight.

But still, she cannot see
Field's steps, shallows and rungs, ends and beginnings, the fence with cows behind it, her grandfather's gable and the wedding below it, the white marquee, her family.

What she can, all she can see, is the crop and the bouncing dot, and so she yells her cousin's name; the word bursts from her like a shot, lodges in the low cloud, sinks into the sky like lead.

And the running head,
changes direction, and only now can Dark discern that it is coming toward her, and only now does she remember that her cousin's polyester plumes are flaxen, that her skin, or rather the liquid powder smoothed across, is toffee, honey, butterscotch; that this day, for the wedding reception, no part of her cousin's complexion is dark like the dot; every part is fair,
that Dark is the cousin who has dark hair. ∎

THE BIRDS OF JUNE

John Connell

The small birds had been at Mrs Mulcahy's window each morning for the last five days. Sitting atop the sill by the open window, they sang out to her bed, never daring to enter the room unless she willed it.

'There's the bold robin,' she said as the dawn light moved across the window and cast a beam by her bedside locker.

She slowly shifted herself upwards, reached towards the top drawer and unfurled the last of the pan loaf.

The birds recognised the crinkle of the grease paper and hopped gleefully towards her. But the robin gave a furtive cry and flew off.

Mrs Mulcahy shrugged and stiffly let some crumbs fall to the floor.

Frances Riordan had watched this procession each morning with great interest; it had become something she looked forward to after the long night-duty shift. She quietly announced herself and moved closer.

'How are you this morning, Nan?'

'Frances, how are you?' she replied, and offered her hand in welcome.

'I see the little fellas are in again,' said Frances, indicating the small birds.

'Ah, but they're great company to me. You'd not tell the matron, would you?'

'It's our little secret, Nan. The matron is never in before eight.'

'I wouldn't want to upset her.'

'No,' agreed Frances.

'You'll have the shift over soon?'

'Another few hours.'

'Any accidents at the casualty?' asked Nan, who liked to be up on the news of the day.

'No, it was a quiet night. We had a small tinker child come in with a bad chest but the doctor sent him home. I didn't have to go down really. Will you have a cup of tea?'

Mrs Mulcahy assented and Frances left the room and walked back down the corridor to the kitchen. The halls were quiet save the sticky peel of her shoes on the lino floor.

Mount Bridget sat at the far end of town, and was made up of the local casualty and the geriatric hospital. The scattering of buildings had been a part of her life for ten years now. Sister Loyola, the matron of the geriatric hospital, had hired her on her return from England with the agreement that she work hard, pray when was needed and treat the patients with respect, helping out with the casualty when required.

They were simple commandments.

Pat, the attendant, was finishing her breakfast when Frances entered the kitchen. The woman stirred from the depths of a faraway thought and smiled a tired smile.

'Nearly there,' she said, and wiped her eyes.

Frances asked that a start be made to the morning teas, and that Pat bring a mug to Nan. She took a place at the staff table and began to fill out the log notes for the previous night. The patients had all slept soundly. Brid Doherty had faded yet again and her breathing grown more shallow. She was returning to her youth with each breath now reminding anyone who listened to make sure her good dress was clean before her daddy came to pick her up. They were off to Leitrim for Monaghan Day.

She had begun to clutch her rosary beads more tightly now, never letting them stray. Exhaling *Ave*s and *Glory Be*s. She would hardly make it to the weekend.

By eight, Frances had begun the breakfast rounds, the milkman had arrived and the morning bustle was under way. Sister Loyola appeared at the staffroom door, quickly looked over the log and invited Frances to join her on her morning round.

'A pleasant night, Frances?'

'It was fine, Matron.'

Sister Loyola's small habit billowed slightly as they walked through the day room. She called on patients who had been ill or fading. Knocking on the door, she would greet them with the early morning. As she lifted a blind or checked a bedpan, she made each feel taken care of.

At Maura Haney's bedside she sat down.

'You're settled now are you, Maura?'

'I am, Matron, surely. The *garl* brought me in a grand cup of tea and toast.'

'And how is the leg?' asked the sister, slowing lifting the bedcovers to examine her amputated limb.

'It's not paining me so much now.'

The matron checked the bandages, gave a gentle sniff and agreed.

'Good, and you'll be sure to come up out of the room today, Maura.'

'For a bit, for a bit,' agreed Maura.

'You need to be out of bed and get some short exercise. I'll have one of the girls come help you later.'

'Thank you, Matron. I'm sorry.'

The sister fixed the bed sheets and the pair left the room.

Those who could rise and walk were escorted to the breakfast hall. Mary-Anne Collins worked quickly in the kitchen to dish out the fried eggs and toast for those who wanted it. She was a great worker though spoke little. She had come from a Magdalene laundry in Limerick as a young woman and had lived among the sisters all her life. There had been a child, though she never spoke of it.

Within the hour they had finished their round.

'It's a comfort when you're on, Frances,' said the matron as they took a breath of fresh air. 'The place is always glowing,' she added and gave her a smile.

'Thank you, Matron.'

The pair enjoyed the calm morning and looked out to see the town slowly come to life. The doctors had arrived at the casualty wing facing the geriatric hospital and the previous night's shift of ambulance men were getting ready to go home and rest. Peter the caretaker was shuffling around the grounds with a ladder under his oxter and a fag in his mouth.

'Were you called down to casualty, Frances?'

'No, there was no ambulances last night.'

'Good. I wish . . .'

'Yes, Matron?'

'I wish the Health Board might find the money to bring in a few more night-duty people. What if when you were on a call we had an emergency here?'

'I thought they said the cutbacks were only for a short time, Matron.'

'That could be years, child. I'll have to bring it up to the Mother Superior when I get a chance.

'How long have you been doing these night shifts now, Frances?'

'Three months, Matron.'

'And do you like it?'

'It's better money and Noel is able to get the children to bed now that they're older.'

'It won't be forever.'

'No, Sister, hopefully not. If the factory takes on a few more people he would be set again. There's not nearly enough for him in the few acres.'

'There never is.'

'God is good, I suppose,' said Frances.

'God is everywhere, but He gave us our lot to do too. Don't forget that.'

Morning Mass was under way as Frances packed her things, clocked out and walked to the car park.

The weekdays were a race to get home and see the children off. The radio was on as she walked in the kitchen and found Noel quizzing the child on her Irish spellings for the day's test.

'Brón,' he said.

'B-R-O-fada-N.'

'Good,' said Noel. 'And what's that?'

'That's sad, Daddy,' said Anne, with a smile on her face.

'And what about this fella? Madra? Can you spell that one?'

'M-A-D-R-A.'

'Mhaith an cailín. It's a scholar we have here, Frances,' said Noel as he gave the child a kiss and packed away her things.

'It's that, all right.'

She picked up the child and gave her a kiss.

'Now spot-check on you and Daddy. Are the teeth washed?'

Anne was silent and turned into her mother's chest.

'Get down and brush them teeth, ya nuck.'

'Where is Con?'

'Just out looking at the new calf.'

'She calved?' asked Frances.

'She did,' said Noel. 'He helped me and all.'

When the children were safely packed in the back of the small Nissan, she drove them to primary school. She was tired now and thought only of her few hours of sleep; a few hours' break from it all.

Noel was out in the fields when she returned. Some porridge had been left out on the table but she could not find the taste on her and instead went straight to bed.

Her dreams were interrupted occasionally by the sound of the cow and her newborn calf from the outhouse sheds. A low bellow would crinkle the folds of her mind and then seconds later it would be answered from some other shed in the distance.

The alarm sounded at two. She began to wash and peel the potatoes Noel had left by the door. Soon the kitchen rattled with the steamy blow of pots and pans. Frances set the table and then returned to the bedroom to get dressed.

It would be another long day. The children arrived home in a flutter of copy books and laughs.

'How was school, Con?'

'Fine,' he said, as he quickly ate the bacon and potatoes she placed in front of him.

'Mammy! I got all my spellings right,' shouted Anne.

'Good girl.'

She looked at them both and smiled. As tired as she was from these nights, the children were worth any effort, any strain.

Noel returned from the fields an hour later and sat down to his dinner.

'How was work, Daddy?' Anne enquired.

'It was fine.'

'Did you get the top fields fenced off from the cows?' asked Con, as he muddled through his maths homework.

'I did. I'll need you to help me get that young heifer over to the rented field.'

'We'll have to borrow the trailer from Uncle Paul, so.'

'We won't. We'll walk her down the road.'

'Didn't she break on us the last time? Can't we get the trailer, Da?'

'We've enough begging and borrowing done for a while. Paul needs that trailer.'

'Sure, what would he mind Da, hasn't he two?'

'I said *no*.'

The boy grew quiet and fixed himself harder on his homework.

'We'll all help you move her, Noel,' said Frances, in an attempt to ease things.

'Aye, might be best.'

'I'll stop the cows,' shouted Anne.

'You'll finish your homework first.'

'It's not that hard anyway, Mammy. I'm nearly done.'

At three the family walked out to the upper ground in search of the lost heifer. Anne wore her bright pink wellingtons, kicking up the dust and puddles as she moved. She ran in fits and stops, excited at the thought of the whole family out in the grass.

Con walked ahead, stooping low and looking at the ground.

'He's growing up isn't he?' Frances said to Noel.

'He is, and getting a mind of his own.'

'You should let him lead her down the road. It'll make him happy to know he's the little man today.'

Noel thought for a moment and nodded in agreement.

They found her in the corner of the garden field, stretched out in the afternoon sun. Ringed around her, the daisies and buttercups were in full bloom. The white down of the thistle flowers floated gently in the air, parachuting their way to new ground.

'Now watch her,' said Noel quietly as he gestured his stick towards the heifer. 'She's a wild bitch. Mammy, you and Anne mind that gap. Con, I'll ring round here and you drive her out.'

The party disbanded and quietly took their places. Anne held Frances's hand as they stood poised and ready.

'Look, Mammy, a flower for you,' said the child, and held up a broken clump of wild broom. The yellow flowers fell to the ground delicately as she waved it in the breeze.

'That's lovely,' she said, and focused her attention on the animal.

Con moved slowly towards her. The heifer gently rose to her feet and with a sudden panic darted for the gap.

'She's coming, Mammy, she's coming!'

The heifer bore down upon Frances in full flight, seeing only the break and opportunity. Frances pushed Anne and began to shout and wave her rubber stick.

The heifer slowed her pace and sniffed at the broken broom and its flowers on the ground.

'She likes it, Mammy,' said Anne, and laughed.

She moved towards the heifer, but at that the beast was gone again, throwing up sods of grass as she galloped through the field. Con moved in behind her now and steadily drove her towards the gate.

'C'mon, hup, hup, ya girl,' he called.

By the second meadow her spirits had calmed and she pushed towards the gate. Noel ran to the road and slowed the oncoming traffic.

Frances took the child's hand and they followed the group.

By Trapp's old house on the corner, the heifer slowed and tore the sweet grass from the verge. Noel ran ahead of the beast. He quietly opened the roadside gate of the rented field and stood ready to turn her in.

Con moved with confidence now and hushed the beast towards his father.

'C'mon, c'mon, that's the girl,' he said, and praised her for her calmness.

'Mammy, I'm tired,' said Anne.

'Hang on, we're nearly there,' Frances said gently.

'I'm tired,' Anne repeated, and stopped walking.

Without taking her eyes from the heifer, Frances picked up the child with a sigh and continued walking. Two cars had gathered to their rear and were waiting patiently for the animal to leave the road. The day was sunny and warm and they did not seem to mind the delay.

Slowly the heifer moved towards the final bend and with a gentle trundle ran into the field and buck-leaped through the grass.

Noel quickly closed the gate and waved the cars on. 'Couldn't have went better.'

'Right enough,' Con replied, imitating his father's style.

The family stood leaning out over the worn gate, gazing at the field and sweet young grass.

'Would you ever buy this field, Da?' asked Con.

'I might,' said Noel, smiling at his wife.

'In time,' Frances said, and ruffled her son's hair.

'And you, were you on this job at all?' Noel said to Anne.

'I was working,' she said confidently.

'Ho ho, I don't know if you were. Didn't I see you trying to give the cow flowers?'

'Those were for Mammy.'

'I think they were for the cow,' said Noel, who picked her up and carried her home, a pink wellington dangling loosely from a foot as the pair joked.

Frances and Con walked back towards the house together. 'You did a right job, Con.'

The boy nodded quietly.

'Daddy will drop you to training this evening,' she said.

'We've the match on Friday.'

'I know. You can call me at work and tell me how it went.'

At home she rested for a time in bed again, counting the minutes before sleep came. She closed her eyes eventually and listened to the children playing in the yard.

Seven o'clock was not long in coming and her alarm sounded again. She washed herself quickly, put on her uniform and applied a layering of light lipstick. Then she walked into the dining room to say goodbye for another night.

The children were watching television and at the sight of her got to their feet.

'You're off, so,' said Noel.

'I am.'

'Mammy, can I call you tonight before bed?' asked Anne.

'You can.'

'Now bed early and don't be acting the bousy on Daddy.' She kissed them both and the family walked her out to the car, waving her off.

The town was littered with tricolours and bunting in ready excitement for the next World Cup match. You could not help but be swept up in the frenzy of it all. She stopped by the Esso station, bought a frozen curry for her dinner and glanced over the day's papers. Jack Charlton smiled out across the headlines. He was a fine man for an Englishman.

The evening sun waned out by the hill of Mount Bridget's as she moved up the driveway. The crows were returning to the rookery.

She signed in and went to see the matron before starting.

'Hello, Matron,' she began, after opening the door.

'Frances, come in,' said Sister Loyola distractedly. She hurried the last of her writing before closing her notebooks. 'Now my child,' she began. 'Is it that time already, another day over?'

'It's that time, Matron.'

'Well let me see, Brid Doherty is very low. I've told the father to be ready to come this evening. The other patients are fine, we had a good few visitors today so the spirits are high.'

'I'm glad to hear that.'

'And the casualty called already. They think they'll be busy in the next few days with the World Cup match, so be on your toes.'

'I will, Matron,' she replied.

'Well that's it all, you know the rest.'

'I do.'

Frances excused herself from the office and made her way to the staffroom to deposit her things in the locker. She left her frozen curry on the draining board. It would be a welcome treat this night, better than any sandwich.

She began to make her rounds, visiting the patients in the day room.

'Ah, Frances, I'm up, see I'm up?' said Maura Haney, gesturing towards her wheelchair.

'Well, that is a welcome sight.'

She sat in the room for a while and enquired of the day's events. The pensions had been paid and the women clutched their handbags close to their chests. Those few pounds made all the difference to their pride.

Peter Cadam proudly walked down the hall in his old black blazer. The new attendant stood and blocked his way.

'I asked the matron, I asked the matron,' he said.

'She didn't tell me,' the girl insisted, making herself wide.

Frances walked towards Peter and touched his shoulder. 'What's the matter, Peter?'

'I asked the matron, and I wanted to go for me pint,' he explained.

'Your pint?'

'You see,' said the young girl, 'he's raving; the matron would never let a patient go out unattended.'

Frances paused and looked at the mockery on the girl's lips. She who tucked the patients in too tight, she who cared not a fig if they wet the bed in the night. She who had no nature.

'I'm sorry to say, Maeve, but Peter can do whatever he pleases, he's here under his own care. Is it Quinn's you're going to, Peter?' Frances enquired.

'It is, just me two pints of a Friday.'

'And Madge is picking you up?'

'She is.'

'Well you tell her I asked for her,' she smiled. 'We'll see you before bed.'

With that, Cadam walked slowly out the hallway and through the front door, leaving the smell of his Brylcreem behind in the air.

Maeve walked away sullenly. She would learn patience, Frances thought. She would learn patience or she would see the road.

By eight the evening tea was served, a simple fried rasher and toast, which none refused.

She called round the various rooms, helping the patients get dressed, cleaning bedpans and turning down covers.

Walking down the corridor she could hear the Bradys call out to one another from across the hall.

'Packey, Packey,' the voice called.

'What do you want, woman?' came the response.

'Are you bringing the cows in this morning?'

'Didn't I bring them in already? It's out from the parlour they'll be going,' he replied.

'That's grand.'

Frances stood in the hallway listening to the elderly couple's chat. It was the same each evening, both as senile as one another. They would never forget home.

She tended Mrs Brady first and found her settling into bed.

'Frances, how are you?' she asked lucidly.

'I'm fine, Mrs Brady. Are you all set for the evening?'

'Yes, yes,' she said, and tucked her purse and rosary beads under her pillow.

'How are the children? We haven't seen Con in an age,' she said.

'He's busy with his father on the farm.'

'A good place to have him.'

Frances helped her adjust her head upon the pillows and placed the blankets around her small frame.

She gave her the tablets and a glass of water to swallow them down.

'Give me a call if you need anything else.'

'I will, I will surely,' she agreed.

As Frances moved towards the door, Mrs Brady turned to her anxiously.

'Will you tell Packey to put the kettle on for the tea?' she said, and with that her sharpness of mind was gone once again.

'I will.'

'Nurse Frances knows you're to have the pot on,' she shouted towards the wall.

'Haven't I it sitting steeping for you?' came Packey's reply a moment later.

Frances smiled and left the room, checked on Packey and continued her rounds. It was a great comfort that they had one another. For no one else called to see them. They were forgotten people, as the matron described them. Forgotten people yes, but they refused to forget themselves.

Frances moved past the oratory and down the single corridor. The evening sun shone through in a glow of red and hazel to illuminate the stained-glass windows and blinds.

Brid Doherty was indeed as low as the matron had said. Her breathing was laborious and strained. Frances wet a cloth and daubed her forehead, cleaning the dried skin from her face. The rosary beads were clutched between her thin fingers and she could pass at any moment. The priest had heard her last confession; there had been little to confess, Frances imagined. A life lived in simplicity in this rural setting. She never had enough money to do the wrong thing.

She wiped her face once again and thought of how she had washed her own children in the same gentle manner. The room took on a quiet calm as Frances watched over her, Brid's chest rising and falling.

Frances sponged her dry lips which now gasped for air, wetting the cracks. It was a scene Frances had experienced many times. Sometimes there had been a fight, a reluctance to let go, but in the end there was always peace.

Brid had no one to sit with her tonight. Her son was on the way from London with his wife, but it might be too late. Frances would come and see her again before the shift was out. And keep a vigil should Brid slip away unseen.

Frances checked her watch and marked the time; it would not be long.

A knock came at the door and she turned to see the face of Mary-Anne Collins.

'A phone call for you, Francie,' said Mary-Anne shyly.

'Can you sit with Brid?'

'But . . . I'm no nurse, what if something happens?'

'It's not a nurse she needs now but company,' explained Frances, and she led Mary-Anne by the hand to the bedside.

'What will I do?'

'It doesn't matter.'

Frances rested a hand on her shoulder to reassure her, then left on her way. The receiver sat off the hook on the staffroom's table.

'Hello.'

'Mammy!' cried Anne.

'Ah hello, and how are you?'

'We're great, Mammy. You said I could call so I wanted to call – is it OK?'

'It's more than fine,' she laughed. 'Is Con back from the match?'

'He is, he's just having a bath.'

'Where's Daddy?'

'He's watching telly. *The Late Late* is on.'

'Oh, very good. You're ready for bed, so?'

'Yeah, but Daddy said I could stay up till half past.'

'So long as you're in bed on the dot.'

'OK.'

'OK, well I have to get back to work now, love.'

The child sighed and agreed, but as Frances moved to replace the receiver her voice came again.

'Oh, Mammy, Mammy,' she said, 'can I go fencing with Daddy and Con tomorrow?'

'Ha, you can. Are you going down to the river, is it? Yeah, well that's fine, but don't go till I'm home.'

'OK, Mammy, I'll tell Daddy,' she said, and shouted off the phone to Noel before returning to the receiver. 'I love you, Mammy.'

'I love you too. I'll see you in the morning.'

'I'll bring in my wellies and have them ready.' She made a kissing noise and ended the call.

Frances decided she'd bring them a few ice creams home in the morning; it would be the weekend after all, they deserved a treat.

As she made to walk out of the room, the casualty alarm flashed amber and sounded off.

The first of the weekend drunks would be coming in, she guessed. She told the young attendant to keep an eye on everything and that she would return in a few minutes.

Though the evening sun was bright and warm, a cool breeze pecked at her feet as she walked down the small hill to the medical building.

There she found the doctor sitting with the tinker family from the night before. The small one lay on the examination table, sweat rolling from his face and chest.

Dr Cullen passed his stethoscope over the child's frame, unbuttoned his faded check shirt and listened to his breathing. The boy did not react at the cold metal upon his skin. He tossed and turned in delirium and began to cough violently.

'What is it, Doctor?' the mother asked in her thick Midlands accent. It was a voice unlike that of the doctors' or anyone else she knew. It spoke of the road and hard living.

'John Paul has pneumonia, I'm afraid,' the doctor said.

'But you said yesterday it was just a chest infection.'

'That was yesterday, and this is today. He's got worse.'

'Well, what's to do for him, so?'

'He needs to be here overnight, but I'm afraid the casualty beds are full.'

The father remained silent and looked adoringly towards his son. A small watery tear in his eye.

'If it's money,' he began, and produced a wad of notes.

'It's not money, Mr Stokes. We don't have a place for him, I'll have to send him in the ambulance to Mullingar Hospital,' said the doctor and gestured away the money.

'He'll go to no hospital, we'll be forgot about up there.'

'I'm afraid that's all we can do.'

'But he's suffering something awful, Doctor, can't we help him now?' Mrs Stokes replied.

Frances moved towards the child, placed her palm on his head and felt the heat of the infection on him. 'I don't think moving him is a great idea, and he can't go home,' she said.

'No,' the doctor agreed.

'What's to be done, what's to be done?' cried Mrs Stokes.

The doctor recoiled in the face of such raw emotion.

'You're a good woman, I can see that,' said Mr Stokes, turning to Frances. 'You've got learning, you can see my son needs help. He needs tablets, medicine. He'll not go home this evening.'

All the room turned to Frances now. She paused and thought. 'And there's really no beds here in casualty?' she asked the doctor.

'None,' he said, and began to pack away his things.

'We'll bring him up to the geriatric hospital,' said Frances.

'To the geriatric?' asked the doctor.

'The child needs a bed and I have one. I'm sure the matron would not mind.'

'Would that be right by you?' she said, turning to the boy's parents.

'That'll be fine by us,' they agreed, and relief swept over their faces.

'We'll bring him up and have a bed made ready for him,' she said.

'John Paul, John Paul,' his father called. 'You've a great *lackeen* to mind you.'

The family carried the child up the hill, refusing a wheelchair. The mother's earrings jangled with each step she took, until they reached the front door of Mount Bridget and quietly followed Frances in. Maeve the attendant stood waiting by the door, smiling.

'I hear we have a sick child,' she said politely.

'We do,' said Frances.

'Blessings on you, nurse,' said Mrs Stokes.

Upon hearing her speak, Maeve's face froze. She called Frances to one side. 'You'll bring no tinkers in here.'

'What?'

'I said you'll bring no tinkers in here.'

'I'll bring whoever I see fit,' said Frances.

'I'll call the matron,' retorted Maeve, 'I don't care what time it is, I'll call her and bring her up here to see this, this clot.'

The child whimpered quietly as the family stood waiting by the doorway.

'I'll serve no tinker, I'll not carry even water to them,' insisted Maeve.

'You've nothing to do with this, Maeve, and I'll remind you, it was the matron who gave you this position and she can as easily take it from you. Now get out of my sight.'

Maeve moved aside and hushed *bitch* under her voice as the family entered the corridor.

The Stokes were quiet as the father placed the boy in the bed.

'The doctor gave me these,' said Mrs Stokes, and handed her some tablets.

Frances examined the bottle and read the label. 'We'll keep the medicine in him and I'll set up a drip for him; he's in need of fluids.'

The parents stood quietly in the middle of the room as Frances prepared the boy, swabbed his arm and inserted the drip.

'Can we stay, Sister?' asked the mother.

'It's Frances, and yes you can, we've broken enough rules this evening, I don't see what else for it.'

'What should we do?' the father asked.

'We'll pray,' said Mrs Stokes.

'If we get him through the night, he'll be fine,' said Frances.

'Would you pray with us?'

'I . . . I don't know,' she began.

'It would mean a lot,' they said.

Frances agreed and they kneeled by the bedside.

Mrs Stokes began:

> *Our gathra, who cradgies in the manyak-norch,*
> *We turry kerrath about your moniker.*
> *Let's turry to the norch where your jeel cradgies,*
> *And let your jeel shans get greydied nosher same as it is where*
>   *you cradgie.*
> *Bug us eynik to lush this thullis,*
> *And turri us you're nijesh sharrig for the gammy eyniks we*
>   *greydied,*
> *Just like we ain't sharrig at the gammi needies that greydi*
>   *the same to us.*
> *Nijesh let us soonie eyniks that'll make us greydi gammy*
>   *eyniks,*
> *But solk us away from the taddy.*
> *Amen.*

She did not know the tinker's language but recognised the Lord's Prayer. She blessed herself as they did and prayed her own silent prayer for the child.

She looked at their worried faces, their devotion so strong and clear; if prayer alone could mend the boy they would need no doctor.

'I should make my rounds,' she said.

'Right you are,' said the father, and turned back to his son.

Frances quietly closed the door and walked back down the corridor. She had hoped to see Nan Mulcahy before bedtime, but the night had worn away and the lights were starting to go out across the wards and corridors.

She walked to Nan's room, gently knocked on the door and opened it to find her sleeping. They would talk in the morning. She would bring her a good strong cup and they would discuss all the news.

By eleven that night, she paused and broke for coffee. Her legs were stiff and she gently massaged her calves as the kettle boiled. When she had her cup in front of her she breathed in the strong aroma, feeling it roll down her throat as she came awake again.

The attendants were cleaning the day room and Maeve was sulking in the canteen. She had no time for the girl now; the matron would deal with her tomorrow.

Tinker or not, he was a child in need. It was nothing but the girl's own backwardness that had blinded her to that.

God is good but He gives us our lot to do.

She looked to her watch and was reminded of Brid Doherty. It had been hours since she had checked on her. She knocked the remains of her coffee over as she stood up quickly and cursed herself as she moved through the wards.

The scene was as she had left it. Mary-Anne sat by the bedside, Brid's hand in hers. She gently stroked it by the pale light of the side table lamp.

'Is everything all right, Mary-Anne? I'm so sorry to have left you for so long; we had a child come into the casualty and I had to bring him here and the time got away and –'

'It's fine,' said Mary-Anne. 'You don't need to be sorry.'

'Is Brid well?'

'Brid is at peace,' she said, and continued to stroke her hand. 'I did not want to leave her, you see. My father always said it was bad luck.'

'Your father was a good man,' said Frances.

She moved towards the corpse and checked the pulse. Her skin was growing cold already.

'She was a good soul,' said Mary-Anne. 'She never treated me any different to the rest, even if I had come from the institution.'

'No,' said Frances. She looked at the time. She would call the priest and get Maeve to lay out the body. Perhaps something of the occasion might wear off on the girl.

'You can go on to bed now, Mary-Anne,' said Frances. She knew the sisters must be wondering what kept her.

'If it's OK, Frances, I'll sit with her a while more. Till the father comes.'

'If you want.'

Frances stroked Brid's face and left the room, closing the door behind her.

The night wore on and finding herself moving towards sleep, she began to clean. She washed the staffroom, cleaning out the presses and cupboards. She heated some water and washed the corridors and wards. It was a way of keeping on, to ensure sleep did not come over her.

The priest arrived from the cathedral and she led him to the room. She left Mary-Anne to talk with him.

Night moved to dawn and now she heated her thawed curry in the oven. Looking out the window, she could see the last of the stars wear upon the sky, twinkle and fade.

The birds would call out soon.

She took a solitary round through the quiet wards and rooms. In the distance, she could hear a low murmur, chanting on and on. She walked further then closer in search of its source and found herself at the door of the tinker boy John Paul's room.

His father and mother sat by the bed. The father was asleep on an old wooden chair and his mother was still steadfastly praying.

The drip was nearly finished and the child looked visibly better. The sun's rays moved slowly into the room, illuminating the scene like a sacred grotto.

A floorboard creaked under Frances's foot and Mrs Stokes looked up from her prayers. 'He's coming back to us.' She ran her hand over her son's face.

'The worst is over,' said Frances. She changed the drip and found the boy's fever was gone.

The child stirred with the pain of the drip's needle and opened his eyes softly, looking around the room and settling on the face of his mother.

'You're getting better, John Paul,' she said.

'Mrs Stokes, will you come have a cup of tea? You've been awake all night.'

'I daren't.'

'I think John Paul is OK now. A cup would do you well.'

The two women walked to the staffroom and Frances prepared a pot. She realised now that they were not so very different: would she herself not spend the night awake by her sick child's bed? Would she not pray furious prayers to see them through safely?

'You're a good woman,' said Mrs Stokes. 'Have you children of your own?'

'Two: a boy and a little girl,' said Frances. 'And you?'

'We've seven,' replied the woman, and laughed. 'I've a lively husband!'

The pair smiled and giggled. The pale colour of the woman's face began to lift as the hot tea brought her back to herself.

'I don't know what we would have done without you this evening. It was God's hand.'

'I'm a mother too,' Frances said simply.

'That you are, and a good one, I'd say.' She stood now and reached out her hand towards Frances. '*Dhalyōn mun'ia,*' she said, and closed her eyes, mumbling unheard words, secret words, and then she blessed herself. 'That's a Traveller blessing,' she explained, 'that's to keep you and yours.'

'Thank you,' said Frances, and she felt a cold tingle run up her back.

'We'll go now,' said Mrs Stokes. 'John Paul is better, as you said yourself. The worst is over him.'

'It is, I did, but I think he should stay on just to be sure.'

The woman shook her head. 'No, no, the morning'll come and there will be too many questions. We don't want to make trouble.'

'But it's no trouble, no trouble at all. The matron is a good woman, a good sister, she won't say anything.'

'Mabye she won't but there are others who wouldn't like us here,' replied Mrs Stokes, and moved out the room and back towards her family.

'But, but . . .' stammered Frances.

They walked back to the room but the child was no longer there.

'Where's John Paul?' Mrs Stokes said, shaking her husband.

'He's here, he's in the bed,' he said, waking up suddenly.

'He's not, he's gone!'

'He can't be gone far; maybe he needed the toilet,' reassured Frances. 'Just wait here, pack your things and I'll find him.'

She moved quickly through the corridors now, checking the washrooms, the oratory – but the boy could not be found. She walked through the ward and saw the pearly lights of dawn on the leather-clad chairs, the flecks of loose skin and dust caught in the slowly moving beams and hovering in the still air.

She began to check the rooms, walking past sleeping patient after sleeping patient. At Mrs Mulcahy's room, she gently opened the old wooden door.

John Paul stood by the open window, with Nan still fast asleep. The small birds gathered round him, the robin perched in his outstretched hand.

He stroked the small bird and it chirped towards him. She stood a moment transfixed.

Nan would never believe it, never.

John Paul turned to her and smiled and with that the robin and his comrades took flight and raced for the window.

The boy's eyes were bright and green, the fight returned to them. She gently led him by the hand back to his worrying parents.

'I found him,' she said, and handed the child back to them. 'You'll need these,' she said, pressing some antibiotics into his father's hands. 'Two of the blue ones in the morning and two of the red ones at night. Keep that up for a week and if he is not better come back to me.'

'Thank you, Sister,' Mr Stokes said, and made again to give her money. His knuckles were thick and worn.

'No, no, there's no need for money. I only wish you'd stay.'

'No, we're better moving,' the mother responded. 'The van is below, John Joe, will you bring it up?'

They walked towards the front door and waited for him to bring up the motor. Frances heard the low cough and splutter of the red Toyota Hiace as it rounded the corner and came to at the foot of the door.

She gently kissed the boy and shook the woman's hand.

'I never got your name,' said Frances.

'It's Margaret,' she said.

They wrapped the boy in another blanket and bundled him into the front seat. Frances waved them off as the sun began to rise up out over the town, past the cathedral and the railroad. In the streets the tricolours and bunting flapped lazily in the breeze, blowing for all they were worth, for everything and nothing. ∎

ALL WE SHALL KNOW

Donal Ryan

Week Twelve

M artin Toppy is the son of a famous Traveller and the father of
my unborn child. He's seventeen, I'm thirty-three. I was his
teacher. I'd have killed myself by now if I was brave enough. I don't
think it would hurt the baby. His little heart would stop with mine. He
wouldn't feel himself leaving one world of darkness for another, his
spirit untangling itself from me.

A t seven weeks or so a foetus starts to move. Imperceptibly,
they say, but I swear I felt a stirring yesterday, a tiny shifting, a
shadow-weight. I've been still and silent all these weeks, listening for
him. I sit here with the curtains drawn and the TV muted, waiting
for a hint of something in the soft glow of things detonating, people
bleeding, corpses being carried swathed in flags by dark-eyed men,
people arguing and kissing and driving in cars, people opening and
closing their mouths.

I've measured his time from the actual minute, not from the first
day of my last period, like a doctor would, where a woman would be
having normal sex, a normal life, and wouldn't know one moment

from another. But all my moments now are marked and measured, standing out in unforgiving light to be examined.

P at came back yesterday evening from weeks of work around the country, installing water meters. They had to stay in digs, he said; the work was round the clock. The day he left he bent and kissed me on the cheek. His lips were cold; he paused before he straightened. I can't remember if I looked at him. That was on the second day of the seventh week.

I stood at the TV-room door last night and looked at him, stretched along the couch in his tracksuit bottoms and Liverpool jersey, barefoot, unshaven, soft-bellied, defenceless. I'm pregnant, I said. He swung his head towards me and there was a sharp light in his eyes – was it maybe joy? – that extinguished itself after a moment, as he remembered. I told him the father was a man I'd met online, in the voice I always use to make him know I'm serious. Low and even.

He sat up, then stood before me, and shouted, JESUS! just once. Then he raised his fists as though to punch me, but he pulled back and punched the air before my face instead, and he said, I'll kill you, I'll kill you, and he put his fists to his eyes and cried, very hard, teeth bared, eyes closed, like a little boy who's just felt shocking pain.

There wasn't much more to be said or done then, so he left. He was white as he walked with his gear bag towards the front door, two small discs of livid red in the centres of his cheeks. He looked back at me from the open doorway. He was ghostly, washed in pale orange light.

Are we even now? His voice was low, almost a whisper. I didn't reply.

I always loved you, Melody Shee, he said.

All I said back was, Goodbye, Pat.

I slept deeply last night, for a while at least. I didn't dream, or if I did I don't remember. My body has started to do its own thing, to do what needs to be done. I'm twelve weeks and two days gone. I announced my pregnancy at the twelve-week mark, as is customary. At twelve weeks the immediate danger has passed, the child has learnt to be, to cling, to grow and grow. Around this time a baby starts to taste. I feel I should be spooning sugar down, to sweeten his world. I tried some ice cream earlier today but it felt too cold in my chest and too hot in my belly, and a few minutes later it came back up. I have a craving now for bacon, wrapped in white bread, with butter and ketchup. He prefers savoury, so.

Pat's father let himself in here sometime in the hour after dawn. I got up and walked around behind him, like a ghost he couldn't see. He took a bagful of clothes from the walk-in wardrobe he'd made for us himself as a first anniversary gift. He took Pat's hurling helmet and togs and boots, and his laptop, and his pile of folders and papers from beside his desk in the small spare room. He left the front door open to ease his quarrying, armful by armful, of his son's life. He forgot the power supply for Pat's laptop so I unplugged it and wound it neatly and handed it to him. He looked at me for the first time. His face was red with anger and embarrassment, and his breathing was heavy and ragged. I wanted to make him a cup of tea and rub his arm and tell him not to worry, and hear him calling me *love* and *sweetheart*, and see him smiling fondly at me, the way he always used to.

I'm sorry, Paddy, I said. I could almost feel his palpitating heart, rippling the air between us. I wanted to tell him to go easy, to mind his poor heart.

Ah, look, he said. Look. And he had no more words for me, nor I for him.

His car was backed into the yard, boot open, engine running. Fumes curled inwards along the hall. I thought, That would be a way to do it. He drove out and stopped on the avenue and walked back to close the gate. Like a protective grandfather, like a man who might say: Better keep that oul gate shut, for fear at all the child might run out in front of a car.

Yesterday's ripple of sickness is a great wave today, rolling in and crashing over me every few minutes. A terrible tiredness came on me this morning and I sat on the couch for most of the day, with a basin at my feet. I rinse it out every now and then, in the kitchen sink.

My muscles ache each time I walk, and my head spins when I get up and when I sit down, and pins and needles prick my goosebumped skin. I don't remember eating, but I must have, because there are crumbs on the kitchen counter, and the rind of an orange.

Morning sickness my arse. The vomiting subsides in the early evening. I slept last night in my dressing gown, cocooned in doubled-over duvets. The air in our room is always cold, except for a few weeks in midsummer. Pat always loved the coldness of the air: he said it made the bed more cosy to have a bit of yourself cold, your toes or the top of your head; you could appreciate being in bed a lot more. Oh, Pat. All the fights fought and terrible words spoken, all the years of nicks and cuts and scattered days when we tore each other so vicious and so deep. And this is what I've done to end it. Announced from the TV-room door that I'd let another man do what you couldn't. I've been on my hands and knees for numberless hours. This is more than I can bear and less than I deserve. We'll slip away to darkness soon enough, and live inside it, just us two, once I have all my loose ends neatly tied.

This morning I stood barefoot on the decking drinking tea. The sickness was gone. I thought about having a fag. My body felt neutral, except for a twitch now and then from the muscles in my abdomen, as though aimless electrons were pulsing along it, shot from some confused gland that had been sleeping up to now. The air was clear and clean and there was a faint smell of mown grass. Someone nearby doing their first cut. I looked at the clay flowerpot at the far corner of the decking that Pat used for years as a giant ashtray, without ever thinking to empty it, overflowing with butts and black muck. My stomach churned a little bit.

I imagined the decking to be a gallows, the wooden planks beneath my feet its trapdoor. An audience of thistles and tufts of grass. I touched the belt of my dressing gown. I thought of the high hook on the bathroom wall. I wondered how long it would take and how much it would hurt. I wondered if there were Stanley blades in Pat's virgin toolbox in the cracked, untreated shed. I thought about a deep bath of roasting water. Why does the bathroom seem to be the natural place? The water and soap and disinfectant, the white tiles on the floor and walls, easily cleaned, the clouding steam. There's something attractive about the dark inversion of leaving the world and curling myself into a cramped, warm space.

I ate: a boiled egg and dry toast. It stayed down. I slept.

Week Thirteen

My days are quadranted neatly now. I wake promptly at eight as I always have. I spend the first hour of each day convinced that I will actually kill myself. I feel relieved. I spend the hour after that worrying about the consequences of killing myself. My relief evaporates. I spend the next hour convinced that I will not kill myself. I feel relieved again. I spend the hour after that worrying about the consequences of not killing myself. My relief evaporates. I repeat this cycle three more times and I go to bed. I sleep for eight hours.

What thread has me tethered to this earth? Fear of pain. And a picture in my head of my father's panicked eyes, having seen the squad car draw up outside with Father Cotter in the passenger seat. His hands shaking as he fumbles with the lock, reaching for the jamb to hold himself upright. His legs buckling in a weakness, big Jim Gildea stepping forward, kind, strong, embarrassed, or a young guard, red-faced and awkward, desperate for their ordeal to be over, catching a hold of him and helping him inside to a chair. A picture in my head of him standing alone at my grave, a cold wind on his face, a look of incomprehension in his eyes, his embarrassment as he accepts the sympathy of friends and barely remembered acquaintances with words that don't sound right in his ears: Thanks; You're very good to come; At least the rain held off; She's in a better place; She's with her mother now. The thought of his aloneness, the completeness of his sorrow, the idea of his world containing nothing, only sadness.

I dreamt last night, one of those dreams that seem so vivid you wake and lie in bed and wonder for a while what's real. I was in a meeting of the Kurt Cobain Club. Breedie Flynn was sitting cross-legged and barefoot in her shorts and I was sitting cross-legged in front of her, watching her. Streams of tears flowed along her cheeks, pooling for moments in tiny valleys formed by acne before falling floorwards. Breedie's face was livid and pitted; Breedie's face was so beautiful I sometimes hated her. We were in Breedie's bedroom in my dream, and we had tented a sheet above our heads between the back of a chair and Breedie's bed, and we had sandbagged ourselves against the world with pillows and cushions and Breedie's collection of stuffed animals from her childhood.

Breedie Flynn and I founded the Kurt Cobain Club in April of 1994. Breedie thought he was a god, I just thought he was gorgeous. Kurt Cobain had chronic stomach pain all of his short life. So did my beautiful friend Breedie. She spoke to a poster of him as though he was in the room; I listened, embarrassed, and I never looked in her face when she almost absent-mindedly held my hand. I liked when she did, though. The Kurt Cobain Club owned these things: a Ouija board we would use to try to summon the spirit of Kurt Cobain; a litre-bottle of vodka we would drink from in terrified sips; a tape recorder and microphone we would use to make recordings of Breedie Flynn's wild stories and imagined conversations in the perfectly mimicked voices of the cool girls, the fellas, the teachers, our parents, with a backing track of my screams of laughter.

Breedie looked at me in my dream and said, Melody, why did you leave me? And she reached for my hand and squeezed it and she was haloed by a blazing light and her hand was burning hot and I woke then, saying, *Breedie, oh, Breedie, I'm sorry,* and lay sweating in the cold air, and felt the creeping nausea hasten to a rush.

M y father rings me every day to tell me things he thinks that
I should know.

He was out at the bottle bank earlier. Someone had a load of
rubbish thrown into it. He said, Lord, isn't it a fright? The CCTV
cameras were broken, of course. I tut into a gap of silence and he goes
on: I met Mossy Shanley yesterday evening below in the hurling field.
The minors lost to Kildangan. Mossy hadn't a good word for poor
old Jack Matt-And. He called him every name you could think of and
a few you'd never think of. You'll have no luck, I told him, speaking ill
of the dead like that. Eff that, says he, and he spat on the ground. Just
because he's dead it doesn't mean he wasn't a bollix. Mossy said that,
imagine. Lord, poor Jack. He hadn't a bad bone. All he ever wanted
was to have a drink and to tell a story. I saw a lad earlier when I was
walking home from devotions, and he driving along and he holding
his telephone to his ear with one hand and he fixing his hair with the
other hand and no hand at all on the steering wheel. Maybe it's a
thing that he had a third hand sprouting from somewhere but if he
had I couldn't see it. I could not.

And he stops and he waits for me to say something back, and he
listens for sadness in my voice, I know.

Will you call over this way one of the days?

I will, Dad.

I know you're busy giving the reading and writing lessons and all.

I am a bit, all right, Dad.

Is it the same little tinker lad you do have all the time?

Traveller, Dad.

Oh, ya, Traveller. Lord, everyone is gone fierce particular about
what they're called these days.

I 'll have to leave the house soon. Time passes as a crawling on my
skin, from my scalp to my soles and back up again. I'll have to
get food, to stay alive while I'm waiting to die, and something for
this sickness. Start of second trimester: morning sickness ends. I
read that in a book, put just like that, set out perfunctorily as a fact,

unassailable, incontrovertible, beneath a photo of a beautiful, smiling, perfect mother-to-be. What if your fucking morning sickness only started at the end of the first trimester? I'd nearly swallow a fistful of Valiums now, just to lie becalmed awhile, and drift away. There's a full bottle on the medicine shelf in the bathroom press. There's vodka in the cocktail cabinet and tonic in the fridge and ice in the freezer. Jesus, the party I could have. Will we do it, little man? I don't know why I'm so sure it's a boy. I just think of the child as the father compressed: red-cheeked and blue-eyed and dark-haired and beautiful. If I'm still alive when this tide of sickness turns I'll go and visit my father.

So here I am still, less sick but no more mobile. Aren't I rightly landed? Forty years ago I'd have been taken bodily away and set to work on the stained vestments of righteous men, the shirts and smocks and socks and smalls of those still in good standing with the Almighty, my baby dragged from me and sold and spirited away to live in grace away from my foulness. I feel a burden of freedom, a cloying sense of open space; I've been sitting now for hours on end unable to rise or to leave this room because I can't think which direction I would turn at the door: away down the hall to bed, or out the door to my car? Where would I go? I have enough money to do me a year or maybe more and this quietness I longed for soon will pass, and everything I wished would end will come crashing to a start again: Pat will bang against the door and beg, and try to make me say I only lied, and I'll open it to the length of the chain and he'll reach through the gap towards me and cry and say, Please, Melody, please. I need you, Melody. Because he always needed me, and still to this day I can't think why.

I could still fly to London and end this, and come back and say, Yes, Pat, I was lying, and he could persuade himself to believe me, and we could take a weekend break somewhere and be massaged together, and walk along a river hand in hand, and stand beneath a waterfall and feel the spray on our faces and laugh, and think about the cave behind the falling water, cut off from the world, and all the roaring peace to be found there, and have a drink in the bar after dinner, and go to bed, and turn to one another's flesh for warmth, and find only a hard coldness there, and no accommodation, no forgiveness of sins; and we'd turn away again from one another, and lie apart facing upwards and send words into eternity about babies never born, and needs unmet, and prostitutes and Internet sex and terrible unforgivable sins and swirling infinities of blame and hollow retribution, and we could slow to a stop as the sun crept up, and turn from each other in familiar exhaustion, and sleep until checking-out time on pillows stained with tears.

Thoughts sharpen themselves on the flints of one another and pierce me like a knife in my middle, sunk deep and twisted around. How we couldn't make ourselves remember, Pat and me. How we loved one other. If only we could have been perfectly dispassionate a moment, viewers from outside, or above, had out-of-body experiences, like floating spirits unshackled from their slashed-open, heart-stopped bodies in a blood-soaked surgery, watching their own evisceration without feeling the pain of it.

He fairly crippled himself, my Pat, with the weight of the expectations of others: his mother, his father, his sister, his friends, his monomaniacal hurling trainers, me. He told me once, not so many years ago, when we were still capable of reason, that he'd never once felt small until he'd met big men. He laughed but he wasn't joking. I watched the tears lay siege behind his eyes. My heart tore for him, it physically pained me. I had no other words, I could only whisper that I loved him, there was that, there'd always be that. And still, even after that, knowing what I knew, having said what I'd said, having wanted so badly to take his pain from him and make it my own, I started only short years later to give my days to making him feel smaller. I waged war against him, and he waged war on me.

You have a fine fat arse for a one that's forever on a diet, he would tell me.

You're like a simple child that's only barely toilet-trained, I would tell him, the amount of piss you get on the floor.

He'd say: A lot you'd know about children, simple or otherwise.

I'd say: You must have a fair shitty seed the way it won't take properly.

He'd say: Why don't you write a poem about it? And send it in to the paper? The way the neighbours can all have a good laugh again. Give the lads below in Ciss's a good howl. Do you know they all read your poems out to each other down there and piss themselves laughing?

I'd tell him he was no man, he was never a man.

He'd tell me I must have a cold cunt of a womb to say no child would stay in it.

I'd call him rotten, and disgusting, and a pervert, and a prick, and I'd roar my throat raw. I'd tell him that I'd never loved him.

He'd tell me in a flat, steady voice that he hated my guts.

How did we turn to such savagery? How did love's memory fade so completely from us? The things we said, the things we thought. My poor Pat, my lovely man, my twinkling boy, my hero. Oh, me, oh, cruel, cruel me, I never knew myself. Tomorrow, I'll have forgotten myself again. ■

THE TRAVELLERS

Birte Kaufmann

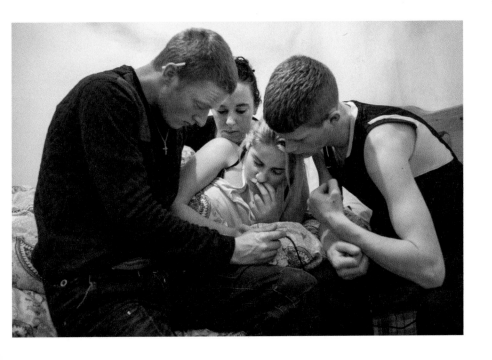

GRANTA

THE MAGAZINE OF NEW WRITING

PRINT SUBSCRIPTION REPLY FORM FOR UK, EUROPE
AND REST OF THE WORLD (includes digital and app access).
For digital-only subscriptions, please visit granta.com/subscriptions.

GUARANTEE: If I am ever dissatisfied with my *Granta* subscription, I will simply notify you, and you will send me a complete refund or credit my credit card, as applicable, for all un-mailed issues.

YOUR DETAILS

TITLE ....

NAME ....

ADDRESS ....

POSTCODE ....

EMAIL ....

☐ Please tick this box if you do not wish to receive special offers from *Granta*
☐ Please tick this box if you do not wish to receive offers from organisations selected by *Granta*

YOUR PAYMENT DETAILS

1) ☐ Pay £32 (saving £20) by direct debit

  To pay by direct debit please complete the mandate and return to the address shown below.

2) Pay by cheque or credit/debit card. Please complete below:

  1 year subscription: ☐ UK: £36 ☐ Europe: £42 ☐ Rest of World: £46

  3 year subscription: ☐ UK: £99 ☐ Europe: £108 ☐ Rest of World: £126

  I wish to pay by ☐ CHEQUE ☐ CREDIT/DEBIT CARD

  Cheque enclosed for £_____ made payable to *Granta*.

  Please charge £_____ to my: ☐ Visa ☐ MasterCard ☐ Amex ☐ Switch/Maestro

  Card No. ☐☐☐☐☐☐☐☐☐☐☐☐☐☐☐☐☐☐☐

  Valid from *(if applicable)* ☐☐ / ☐☐   Expiry Date ☐☐ / ☐☐   Issue No. ☐☐

  Security No. ☐☐☐

SIGNATURE .... DATE ....

Instructions to your Bank or Building Society to pay by direct debit

BANK NAME ....

BANK ADDRESS ....

POSTCODE ....

ACCOUNT IN THE NAMES(S) OF: ....

SIGNED .... DATE ....

DIRECT Debit

Instructions to your Bank or Building Society: Please pay Granta Publications direct debits from the account detailed on this instruction subject to the safeguards assured by the direct debit guarantee. I understand that this instruction may remain with Granta and, if so, details will be passed electronically to my bank/building society. Banks and building societies may not accept direct debit instructions from some types of account.

Bank/building society account number
☐☐☐☐☐☐☐☐

Sort Code
☐☐☐☐☐☐

Originator's Identification
9 1 3 1 3 3

Please mail this order form with payment instructions to:

Granta Publications
12 Addison Avenue
London, W11 4QR
Or call +44(0)208 955 7011 Or visit
GRANTA.COM/SUBSCRIPTIONS for details

Literary Review

FOR PEOPLE WHO DEVOUR BOOKS

3 issues for only £5 + a free *Literary Review* tote bag.

Sixty-four pages of witty, informative and authoritative reviews each month by leading contemporary writers and thinkers *plus* free access to our app, website and online archive dating back to 1979. Visit us online at **www.literaryreview. co.uk/3for5** for more.

Your free tote bag will ship when you automatically continue on to a direct debit subscription for the special rate of £32 per year. UK/direct debit only. International readers instead use code OVERSEAS for a discount of over 20%.

www. literaryreview. co.uk/3for5

A VISIT TO THE ZOO

Colm Tóibín

When Heinrich made his first visit to his father in the hospice and asked him if he wanted anything, his father merely requested some philosophy books. He was not sure, the old man whispered as he tried to sit up in bed, that he would be able to read them, but nonetheless, he would like to have them close. He pointed to the flowers that were beginning to wither in a vase on the bedside locker beside a jug of water and a glass tumbler.

'Instead of the flowers,' he said in a stronger voice, 'I would like to see the books if I wake in the night, or perhaps even reach over and touch one of them. Or maybe I would like to expire with them in easy reach.'

When Heinrich asked him which books he wanted, his father gave a tiny shrug.

'The ones that matter. And some new ones that are on the desk, the ones I was going to read before they took me here.'

His father's two-room apartment was in the Soviet-style block of Humboldt University normally used to house visitors. It had none of the clutter of the large, light-filled apartment on Martin Luther Strasse in Munich where Heinrich's parents had lived for most of their married lives, with paintings on the walls and philosophy books piled up in the hallway and the living room as well as the study and his father's side of the bed in his parents' bedroom.

Once his father had decided to move to Berlin when his mother died, most of the paintings in the Munich apartment were sold and most of the books given away. His father wished, as he put it, to take part in the new Germany by working in a university that had been in the former East. In the press interviews he gave at the time, he stressed that he would be moving without many possessions, almost like a monk entering a monastery. But unlike a monk, he added, he would spend his last frugal years in the knowledge that truth existed but would remain, for the moment, enticingly beyond his grasp. His search for it would be merely an act of homage to the numinous, the ineffable, the mysterious and ungraspable core of things.

As expiation for his former life, he also explained, he would keep his two modest, dimly lit rooms in Berlin almost bare. In one room there was merely a low table for a stereo and a shelf above it for some CDs; there was one easy chair and a small table. A Paul Klee drawing was the sole piece of decoration on any of the walls. As Heinrich stood in his father's apartment now and looked at the Klee drawing, he wondered if drawing was really the word for this piece; it was merely a few lines in pencil, little gestures that could not have taken much time. Or maybe they took more time and consideration than anyone imagined. This was the sort of paradox that had always amused his father, and perhaps, Heinrich thought, still amused him now while he lay dying in the hospice, the place where he had insisted he would not go, until the pain in his back grew too severe for him to remain in this apartment.

Since the doctor who came to visit him here had refused to accede to his request for enough morphine to put an end to himself in one brisk gulp, as his father had phrased it, his father finally had no choice but to allow himself to be taken to the hospice and be, as he ruefully said, let die slowly in an environment that was calm and antiseptic and full of smiles, like he supposed heaven would be, or, he added, hell, or some strange space in-between that no one had yet named.

It was easy for Heinrich to locate the books because his father's study, with a low single bed in the corner, was even more spartan than the sitting room. Plato, he thought, that would have to come first. He almost laughed at the memory of himself as a fifteen-year-old reciting by heart a passage from the *Symposium* to his parents, only to be told by his mother that his father, in fact, knew it by heart in the original Greek. This was a lesson, he realised, that many boys of his age had shared – the lesson that there is always someone unfailingly better than you, and someone else, bound to the first in marriage, who is ready day and night to proclaim proudly that you will never, no matter how hard you try, be equal to the one who came before you, your only begetter. His father, his mother was always ready to insist, was the substantial one; the son, despite being mostly lovable, was merely a shadow, if also her favourite boy in the world.

Maybe it was that sharp sense of his own inadequacy and his own insubstantiality and pale lovability, Heinrich thought, which had provoked him into becoming a novelist, someone who lived most usefully when unnoticed, confidently imagining lives for others, rather than trying to follow his father who had become a public figure in post-war Germany, a teacher admired and revered by students, a man in regular and highly publicised contact with both Willy Brandt and Angela Merkel while they were in office. His father managed to make clear that he simply had not seen the chancellors in-between because he did not deem them worthy of his attention.

His father had loved opposites; he made distinctions between things that a less fine mind might have connected. His great subject was duality; he was the high priest of things that were irreconcilable. Heinrich, on the other hand, was more at home with chaos, with narratives that imposed on each other, with fictions that allowed in more than one voice, more than one perspective, more than one time period. Maybe, it struck him now, with parents like his, and the amount of time he had spent alone as he was growing up, that the noise he made when he wrote – and indeed the silence – and the connections he made between things were a natural response to his upbringing. He needed to find points of intersection, links.

His parents' gift to him, then, he thought, was the life of his imagination, a life bathed in the rich poetics of merging narratives and a sense of irony about the whole idea of Being and Consciousness. During his upbringing, he had a sharp and persistent sense that his presence, or his being alive at all, was never entirely necessary, and that he could have easily and more successfully been someone else or no one. This, in turn, created the bedrock for a feeling he had that every choice he made had a shadowy alternative, that every novel he wrote had other novels lurking within its narrative shape, that every thought or decision had a sweeter sibling, and also the impression that every woman he met had a ghostly sister or cousin or colleague, or indeed a friend, standing close to her, who was more alluring, more intelligent, more filled with calm understanding, more serene, more close in her own precise desires to fulfilling his shifting ones.

Thus each time he thought about Lisa, to whom he had been married now for two years, he was never fully sure about her, although when he actually saw her – in that second, for example, when she appeared to meet him in a restaurant or a cafe, or when he watched her coming in the door of their apartment, or when she was sitting in an armchair reading – then she became substantial, essentially known to him. But this sureness about her and this knowledge could fade when they were halfway through supper, or when he woke in the night when she was still sleeping, or in the morning when she was hurrying and slightly short-tempered. At those times, she could seem like someone he barely knew, almost alien in her otherness. She was sixteen years younger than he was; he wondered if that made a difference to how they connected, and he supposed that it did.

He wondered too if he was alone in the extent of this constant emotional wavering. Since he had never read a good, sharp, accurate account of the mixed feelings he suffered, he wondered if he should not try to write about these feelings, even in diary form, or maybe better describe them in a novel. Or maybe better still, or wiser, since Lisa read every word he wrote, find a metaphor for them, or hand them over to one person, or a set of figures, who had lived in an earlier century, or who might live in the future.

His father, he thought, had loved his mother because she was no one else, and he had harboured no feelings, as far as Heinrich knew, that somehow things might have been different or better if he had married another woman, or left his wife years ago for a bright young student, as so many of his colleagues had done. His parents, it struck him, were so united in his father's view that the world is made up of single things correctly placed and shaped, a line of stand-alone decisions, they were so steeped in the art of certainty and inevitability, that they had failed to imagine another life for themselves. Nonetheless, they were glad, he felt, that their sense of singularity had not been passed on to him, their only child, as though teaching him to follow them in their beliefs might have become a way of diluting them, lessening them. They were a selfish pair, he thought, and he was glad he was no longer under their sway.

At least glad until now, now that he had to visit his father every day in the hospice, oversee his care and imagine a time when he would be completely without his father, having lost his mother years before.

While he watched his father dying, he felt indeed under his sway once more, as if he had previously been a student freed for holidays and was now, as he tried to complete a thesis, back under the severe watch of a famously exigent professor.

Unlike his parents, then, he himself lived in a miasma of wondering if things could have been otherwise. In his novels, he applied what he did and did not know to science and to espionage, as much as to romance or the paradoxes of history. This meant that his books were read by men as well as by women. Indeed, his way of dramatising the cloud of unknowing seemed to appeal more to men, especially in the Germany of the 1990s, but it also made his own dream life, his immersion in irony and illusion, richer sometimes than his actual life with Lisa. His vast longings and dreamings made his life with her difficult sometimes. Maybe, he thought, it made her life with him difficult as well, but she was, he felt, too practical and self-protective to let such things bother her too much. But it was hard to be sure.

As he looked through his father's shelves now, he noticed the books his father had written on both Wittgenstein and Heidegger. His father, he knew, had relished the very presence of these two philosophers in the world, because the chasm between them could not be filled. This embracing of each separate thing for its own absolute and solid quality, the refusing to allow for the possibility that things might, under pressure or in time, merge, disappear, dissolve and change shape, was perhaps a way for his father to keep at bay the stark simplicity of being forced through illness and weakness and age to float into eternity.

In all his books and essays and reviews and lectures, Heinrich realised, his father had never mused on our final journey towards the undiscovered country. Whatever the origins of his philosophical position, Heinrich thought as he sat at his father's desk, his father's fascination with irreconcilable dichotomies, with the gaps within arguments, his insistence on the stability and immutability of all concepts, his refusal to allow thesis and synthesis to become anything other than themselves, his lifelong struggle against the protean and the dialectic, were being fought out now within his ailing body and would end soon. He would, as a metaphysician might put it, become pure soul, mere spirit, within a short time. All speculation would end for his father once his brain was denied oxygen. It was as simple as that. His father, Heinrich knew, was struggling with the novel concept that shortly there would remain, at least for him, no further distinctions to be made. Death would make everything the same.

'Thesis, antithesis, corpse,' Heinrich whispered to himself and stood up again to look through the rows of books about philosophy, smiling as he noticed his father's own book *Against Metaphysics*, long out of print.

He found a well-used edition of *The Critique of Pure Reason* on an upper shelf and put it beside a compendium of Heidegger's essays, and then found the *Tractatus* and a heavily annotated edition of *The Structural Transformation of the Public Sphere*, before examining what was on the desk itself. He flicked through a big volume by Peter

Sloterdijk, which looked unread, and a book in English still in its cellophane package called *On What Matters* by Derek Parfit, which was new to him. He put them all in a heavy plastic shopping bag. Since his father could die at any time, it was best, he thought, to take these books to him as soon as possible.

They would be unusual presences in a hospice for the dying, and in their bulk and because of the smell of dust from a few of them, and in their variety and complexity, they might irritate the nurses, who liked to keep things small and soft and simple and antiseptic for the patients in their last painless days under their care, a care which took no notice of the great and bitter disputes that had gone on between philosophers about ethics or epistemology or being-in-the-world, or the conclusions, both tentative and grand, which these men had come to about the shape and meaning of society or indeed existence.

When they knew each other first, he had kept Lisa away from his father. Once she had moved in with him, he had not mentioned to his father that he was living with his girlfriend. When Lisa had answered the phone to his father a number of times, however, the two had begun to communicate. He remembered a few times standing coldly by the phone waiting for Lisa to stop chatting idly to his father, laughing and smiling. When he and Lisa got married, Heinrich did not even tell his father. While some of Lisa's family and a few of their friends had attended the modest civil ceremony, Heinrich had insisted that his father was not well enough to do so. But slowly, by careful management, Lisa found a way to be included in the visits to his father, which soon became outings to various new restaurants in the city, the meals paid for each time by his father, who behaved with old-fashioned courtesy to Lisa, remembering each thing she said about her studies in the art college and the beginnings of her career as a designer. Heinrich grew to find these outings useful because the old intensity of being ignored by his father gave him deeply rooted images for the book he was working on. But he also found the trips infuriating and was glad each time when they dropped the old man back to his spartan quarters in the guest house of Humboldt

University and his life alone contemplating truth, or the dry version of it which he had distilled.

He should, he thought, have been able to predict that his father and Lisa would bond in the hospice, that the old man, filled up with morphine, would need someone at whom to direct his charm. Lisa held the patient's hand and, when he fell asleep, sat watching him fondly. If he woke and found only Heinrich there, his father would turn away. Once Lisa was there, however, he brightened up and began to talk to her, asking about the news of the day and requesting that she read to him from the newspaper. As Heinrich sat watching them he moved from feeling proud of Lisa's tact and warmth to feeling an immense rage at both of them, and wishing his father had spared him this parting message that his presence was not quite required, and wishing also that Lisa would stop flirting with the old man, and, in fact, would stop wanting to visit him at all and would also stop suggesting that she was responsible for him, a part of her family now that she had married Heinrich. As his father and Lisa chatted easily and warmly about Angela Merkel's dress sense or tone of voice, or their mutual dislike of Austrians, Heinrich wished that he had not married Lisa, or had made clear to her from the start of his father's illness that she should not feel that she had to visit him, and that she should not become implicated in his father's effortless suggestion that his son could be easily ignored and somehow did not matter unless he was needed for a second to call a nurse or fetch a cold drink from the shop in the lobby. Heinrich found it hard to know what to say when Lisa remarked one evening on leaving the hospice that his father was a wonderful man, a truly great figure, facing death with such serenity and insouciance, and that Germany would be a poorer place without him when he died. Heinrich did not think he could tell her that his father was not facing death at all, and his talking to Lisa about the most mundane matters and his charming her with his fake stoicism were merely a way of creating the pretence that he was not about to go down into the dark.

One early afternoon as they were getting ready to visit, when Lisa said that they would need to take an overcoat and scarf for his father, Heinrich wondered if she had developed a black sense of humour in the face of his father's illness.

'I don't think he'll be going anywhere. Or at least not anywhere where he will need a coat and a scarf,' he said.

'He wants to go to the zoo,' Lisa replied.

'To be fed to the lions?'

'Stop it! They asked him if there was anything he wanted to do. We discussed it and he said he would like to visit the zoo, so a nurse is going to come with us.'

'My father has no interest in the zoo.'

'He does now.'

'When did he say this?'

'After you had left early yesterday, the doctor asked him if there was anything he wanted to do. It is all arranged.'

'The zoo? Are you sure?'

'And he wants us to come with him. Both of us.'

Heinrich wondered if it was the effect of the morphine, or if it was another way of postponing the realisation for his father that his time was coming to an end. It seemed, in any case, oddly frivolous for a man steeped in Plato and Aristotle, Spinoza and Kant, to wish to go to the zoo in Berlin and, as his last act in the world, peer at animals in captivity. Maybe, Heinrich thought, his father was returning to a sort of infancy or an adolescence that he had never, in fact, known. As the son of a Lutheran minister who had been appalled by Hitler, his father had not had an easy childhood, and when he was nine the war began. So it was unlikely, Heinrich imagined, that he had, years before, enjoyed many days out at the zoo.

At the hospice, the staff seemed almost excited at the prospect of a patient who wished to go out into the world one last time. The wheelchair was ready, and the nurse who would accompany them had a list of what they would need to take with them. The doctor on duty appeared ready to marvel at the idea that his father would travel in an ordinary taxi in the company of Heinrich, Lisa and the nurse, with the wheelchair in the boot. The only question was: should the taxi wait for them in a nearby side street, or should they travel to the zoo in one cab and then attempt to hail another on the street for the return journey? When Heinrich drily suggested that they should ask the driver to wait for them, that, at this point, the cost of a taxi was something they should not worry about, the doctor nodded in satisfaction. There was something, however, about the doctor's demeanour – the deep concern mixed with a kindly competence and a small edge of saintliness – that made clear to Heinrich that he should not dream of using this opportunity to ask how long his father was likely now to live. Such banal questions belonged to the real world, and the hospice was, more than anything, a respite from the real world, an ark floating freely against the factual, helped by church-like silence, soft furniture, pastel colours, a smiling staff, large doses of morphine for the patients and a discreet side door for coffins.

His father, dressed but badly shaved and in his wheelchair, had the strained and fearful look of someone who had been released from prison after a long sentence. Heinrich almost wanted to hold his hand, or touch his shoulder, but such a display of tenderness, he thought, would let his father know how frail and pitiful he seemed. Lisa did all the managing and talking as the nurse wheeled his father towards the taxi waiting at the entrance. Heinrich walked behind and wondered how his father, who would know that this was likely to be his last outing as a living, sentient being, was going to feel when they arrived back to the hospice, back to the cushioned house of death, with the world and all its mysteries in dark abeyance. He felt sorry for his father, and almost proud of him for wanting, on this winter day, one last look at the world. He stood back and watched, as his father seemed to enjoy the attention of both Lisa and the nurse as they helped him into the front seat of the taxi and made sure that he was comfortable.

'Has anyone asked him what he wants to see in the zoo?' Heinrich whispered to Lisa as, having arrived in front of the zoo, they were taking the wheelchair from the boot of the car.

'He wants to see the aquarium as well, and so we have to buy tickets for both. I checked online.'

'Fish?'

'There must be some reason.'

The light was grey and there was a sense, Heinrich felt as he followed his father through the entrance, that the world was an old place with tired skies and tired cities beneath them and an exhausted countryside stretching into the distance. He was glad that it was not summer; there was no need for bright chatter. And he was glad, too, that they had come to this place where animals were held against their will rather than some well laid-out park with a stream running through it, or the bank of a river somewhere. This was grim, tawdry nature caught in the middle of a city rebuilt after aerial bombing, a city which, despite its best efforts and many marketing plans and provision of cheap housing for artists, had lost its essence and would never get it back again.

When they heard the roar of what sounded like a lion, Heinrich's father indicated that they should move towards that sound. Once they found the set of rocks and railings, they saw a single lion prancing proudly up and down a jagged territory as though this were its domain. His father indicated first that he wanted the brake put on the wheelchair so that he could contemplate the roaming animal. This must be, Heinrich thought as he studied the lion too, what a lion looked like, this must be how it moved, full of muscle and power and sharp belligerence. But if he were told that it was, in fact, virtual, something stuffed and mechanised and staged for visitors, Heinrich would not have been surprised. The lion looked like a parody of a lion; its movements and its way of smelling the air and then guiding itself towards some definite prey ahead had all the appearance of parody. The joke, of course, was on the lion, were it indeed real, but it was also on anyone watching, especially on anyone watching as fiercely as his father, as if the lion would yield some fresh truth about creation or evolution or the power of the indomitable will.

After a while, when the nurse insisted that they should move, they went into a heated building where there were high cages with colourful birds from Asia and Africa and Australia and South America flying around. His father, Heinrich thought, was almost like a bird too, as he gazed at each species. He looked like he might consider flying out of the wheelchair and through the Perspex wall to gobble one of them up. When they stopped in front of a cage that had a large yellow bird flitting elegantly from branch to branch, his father pointed at the bird. He stopped and seemed to be thinking, before trying to look around to find Heinrich. When Heinrich noticed this, he knelt down so that his father could more easily speak to him.

'Yellow,' his father said. 'Yellow. Goethe said that colour was troubled light, but I don't think so. It might have been a passing remark of his. I think colour is colour. I mean, there has to be colour. Otherwise, there would be nothing, or just blankness and voices and the feel of things on your skin. I don't think any of us has ever paid enough attention to colour. Aristotle thought there were only two colours. You'd wonder if he had eyes in his head. But maybe his eyes were too full of what was going on in his head. Like the rest of us. Not looking enough. No one has ever looked enough.'

He nodded sadly and looked at the yellow bird again.

Between the bird sanctuary and the aquarium they passed a group of penguins caged in a zone where there was fake snow falling. They stood in a group like people busy consulting each other, managing, Heinrich thought, to seem both placid and preoccupied at the same time, like good capitalists or tenured philosophers.

'They look like a group of philosophers,' he said. 'At the coffee break during a conference.'

His father did not seem to hear him. Lisa and the nurse ignored him as they pushed the wheelchair towards the aquarium. When his father made as though to speak, Heinrich moved forward so that he could hear him. They stopped the wheelchair.

'If there are snakes in here,' he said, looking at Heinrich directly, 'then I don't want to see snakes. I like their symbolic value, and their use as metaphor also of course, but I don't want to see them wriggling around on their bellies, and I want to be spared sight of their terrible tongues, if tongue is the word for what snakes have in their mouths, if mouth is the word for that opening they have under their eyes.'

'What do you want to see?' Heinrich asked.

'Fish. The fish that cling to the bottom. The primitive beginning of things. Organisms that are easily satisfied. The ones who keep out of trouble. I wonder if keeping out of trouble is not the real thing. Maybe that is what thinking is, or should be – a way of keeping out of trouble. Maybe we could learn from fish, the ones who don't get eaten, that is. The main thing, I suppose, is not to get eaten. At least when you are alive. Yes, not to get eaten.'

His father spoke like a man about to embark on a new book, who had to consult widely. It struck Heinrich now that this was what the morphine was doing. It was not just masking the pain, which had been severe, but it was entering into his father's spirit and filling him full of purpose. His wish to visit the zoo arose indeed from something serious, but it was seriousness operating at one strange remove from itself, as a voice slightly out of tune can go on singing, or a camera lens out of focus can still take a picture. His father sounded as he had always done during the writing of a book. This was the sound that Heinrich knew best, even when it was silent. When he was in the full of his health, however, his father's projects were feasible and always completed, with many pages of footnotes. He was famous, in fact, for his footnotes, their rigour and often their length. Now the idea that he was writing a new book about not getting eaten seemed to fire his ambitions and preoccupy him as much as in the past he could become preoccupied for a year or more about matters in the history of thinking which could, in his opinion, never be properly reconciled.

As they moved down the gallery, they stopped when they came to the chameleons. The two chameleons in a glass case appeared to interest all of them, Heinrich thought, because of their beauty and their stillness. They looked like a pale painting. It would not matter to the chameleons, Heinrich felt, if they faded away. They could easily merge with things, unlike humans, he thought, whose ungainly bodies have to be burned or buried in the earth, and who have property to be disposed of, clothes to throw out. Ideas.

His father seemed transfixed by the chameleons and put up his hand demanding silence when he thought that someone was going to speak. He signalled to Heinrich to come close. And when he did, he signalled to him further to remain still and watch. There was a small insect, like a cockroach, moving slowly along a branch within the glass case where the two chameleons were. It had eyes and a mouth that could be clearly seen. The chameleon on the closest branch was placidly gazing at it, in a pose of unconcern. Nothing happened as the insect moved slowly forward; it was blindly approaching the chameleon. The insect's main effort, it appeared, was not to fall over. It was difficult to imagine, Heinrich thought, where it presumed it was going, or why.

Suddenly, without moving, or making any obvious effort, the chameleon put out its long tongue and rolled the insect into its mouth, a mouth too small to take in the captured object in one gulp, so that for a few moments minuscule, wriggling legs or tentacles stuck out of the chameleon's mouth. And then the insect was gone. It was as if it never had been.

Perhaps, Heinrich thought, it had left little insects with its own genetic code wandering in some other part of the zoo, or freely on the earth, but otherwise there was no sign anywhere that there had once been an insect, this particular insect. His father nodded his head, not exactly in approval of what he had witnessed, but in seeming confirmation of what he had suspected all along. And then he signalled that they should move on.

When they arrived at the jellyfish, Heinrich's father reached into an inner pocket and took out his reading glasses and put them on. With his finger in the air, he began to follow the wavering movements of a tiny jellyfish in the water on the other side of the glass, or what appeared to Heinrich more like a particle of a jellyfish, or an embryo, or a section of an embryo. All four of them watched, as the tiny jellyfish resisted and then accepted the current of the water in the tank. It was more like a parachute than a fish, Heinrich thought, and its colour was closer to no colour at all than blue or pink, even though there were traces of blue and pink in the bell-shaped film above a small amount of matter that pulsed as it floated.

'Pulse, heart, vagina,' his father said in a loud, authoritative voice.

He indicated then that he wanted to go. The nurse assented and lifted the brake on the wheelchair. Lisa walked ahead, checking regularly that the old man had been satisfied with his visit to the aquarium, while the nurse, who had not spoken once, but had remained competent, gentle and fully in control, pushed the wheelchair. Heinrich walked behind feeling a strange new sadness about his father and his sudden mania for looking at these abject creatures in captivity, and making statements about them, statements that sounded as if they were making sly fun of all his life's work. Heinrich silently repeated the words 'pulse', 'heart' and 'vagina', but they were his father's words, and they must have been of some use to his father, perhaps he had spoken them out loud to keep other, more menacing, or terrifying, words, out of his mind. But they were of no use to Heinrich now as his father and he and Lisa and the nurse made their way back in the taxi through the Berlin traffic to the hospice. Before, such words might have made him laugh, but the time for laughter, it struck him, was, at least for the moment, suspended. ∎

THE WONDER

Emma Donoghue

I n her dream the men were calling for tobacco, as always. Underfed, unwashed, hair crawling, botched limbs seeping through slings into stump pillows, but all their pleas were for something to fill their pipes. The men reached out to Lib as she swept down the ward. Through the cracked windows drifted the Crimean snow, and a door kept banging, banging –

'Mrs Wright!'

'Here,' Lib croaked.

'A quarter past four, you asked to be waked.'

This was the room above the spirit grocery, in the dead centre of Ireland. So the voice in the crack of the door was Maggie Ryan's. Lib cleared her throat. 'Yes.'

Once dressed she took out *Notes on Nursing* and let it fall open, then put her finger on a random passage. (Like that fortune-telling game Lib and her sister used to play with the Bible on dull Sundays.) Women, she read, were often more *exact and careful* than the stronger sex, which enabled them to avoid *mistakes of inadvertence.*

But for all the care Lib had taken yesterday, she hadn't managed to uncover the mechanism of the fraud yet, had she? Sister Michael had been there all night; would she have solved the puzzle? Lib doubted it somehow. The nun had probably sat there with eyes half closed, clacking her beads.

Well, Lib refused to be gulled by a child of eleven. Today she'd have to be even more *exact and careful,* proving herself worthy of the inscription on this book. She reread it now, Miss Nightingale's beautiful script: *To Mrs Wright, who has the true nurse-calling.*

How the lady had frightened Lib, and not only at first meeting. Every word Miss N. pronounced rang as if from a mighty pulpit. *No excuses,* she'd told her raw recruits. *Work hard and refuse God nothing. Do your duty while the world whirls. Don't complain, don't despair. Better to drown in the surf than stand idly on the shore.*

In a private interview, she'd made a peculiar remark. *You have one great advantage over most of your fellow nurses, Mrs Wright: you're bereft. Free of ties.*

Lib had looked down at her hands. Untied. Empty.

So tell me, are you ready for this good fight? Can you throw your whole self into the breach?

Yes, she'd said, *I can.*

Dark, still. Only a three-quarter moon to light Lib along the village's single street, then a right turn down the lane, past the tilting, greenish headstones. Just as well she hadn't a superstitious bone in her body. Without moonlight she'd never have picked the correct faint path leading off to the O'Donnells' farm, because all these cabins looked like much of a muchness. A quarter to five when she tapped at the door.

No answer.

Lib didn't like to bang harder in case of disturbing the family. Brightness leaked from the door of the byre, off to her right. Ah, the women had to be milking. A trail of melody; was one of them singing to the cows? Not a hymn this time, but the kind of plaintive ballad Lib had never liked.

> But Heaven's own light shone in her eyes,
> She was too good for me,
> And an angel claimed her for his own,
> And took her from Lough Ree.

Lib pushed the front door of the cabin and the upper half gave way.

Firelight blazed in the empty kitchen. Something stirring in the corner: a rat? Her year in the foul wards of Scutari had hardened Lib to vermin. She fumbled for the latch to open the lower half of the door. She crossed and bent to look through the barred base of the dresser.

Stepping back, Lib almost tripped on something white. A saucer, rim poking out from beneath the dresser. How could the slavey have been so careless? When Lib picked it up, liquid sloshed in her hand, soaking her cuff. She hissed and carried the saucer over to the table.

Only then did it register. She put her tongue to her wet hand: the tang of milk. So the grand fraud was that simple? No need for the child to hunt for eggs, even, when there was a dish of milk left out for her to lap at like a dog in the dark.

Lib felt more disappointment than triumph. Exposing this hardly required a trained nurse. It seemed this job was done already, and she'd be in the jaunting car on her way back to the railway station by the time the sun came up.

The door scraped open, and Lib jerked around as if it were she who had something to hide. 'Mrs O'Donnell.'

The Irishwoman mistook accusation for greeting. 'Good morning to you, Mrs Wright, and I hope you got a wink of sleep?'

Kitty behind her, narrow shoulders dragged down by two buckets.

Lib held up the saucer – chipped in two places, she noticed now. 'Someone in this household has been secreting milk under the dresser.'

Rosaleen O'Donnell's chapped lips parted in the beginnings of a silent laugh.

'I can only presume that your daughter's been sneaking out to drink it.'

'You *presume* too much, then. Sure in what farmhouse in the land does there not be a saucer of milk left out at night?'

'For the little ones,' said Kitty, half smiling as if marvelling at the

Englishwoman's ignorance. 'Otherwise wouldn't they take offence and cause a ruction?'

'You expect me to believe that this milk is for the fairies?'

Rosaleen O'Donnell folded her big-boned arms. 'Believe what you like or believe nothing, ma'am. Putting out the drop of milk does no harm at least.'

Lib's mind raced. Both maid and mistress just might be credulous enough for this to be the reason why the milk was under the dresser, but that didn't mean Anna O'Donnell hadn't been sipping from the fairies' dish every night for four months.

Kitty bent to open the dresser. 'Get out with ye, now. Isn't the grass full of slugs?' She hustled the chickens towards the door with her skirts.

The bedroom door opened and the nun looked out. Her usual whisper: 'Is anything the matter?'

'Not at all,' said Lib, unwilling to explain her suspicions. 'How was the night?'

'Peaceful, thank God.'

Lib went into the little room, turning sideways to let Sister Michael out.

Anna made the sign of the cross and got up off her knees. 'Good morning, Mrs Wright.'

Lib shut the door behind her. She considered the girl with grudging respect. 'Good morning, Anna.' Even if the girl had somehow snatched a sip or a bite of something during the nun's shift, it couldn't have been much; only a mouthful, at most, since yesterday morning. 'How was your night?' Lib got out her memorandum book.

'*I have slept and have taken my rest,*' quoted Anna, crossing herself again before pulling off her nightcap, '*and I have risen up, because the Lord hath protected me.*'

'Excellent,' said Lib, because she didn't know what else to say. Noticing that the inside of the cap was streaked with shed hair.

The girl unbuttoned her nightdress, slipped it down and tied the sleeves around her middle. A strange disproportion between her fleshless shoulders and thick wrists and hands, between her narrow chest and bloated belly. She sluiced herself with water from the basin. *'Make thy face to shine upon thy servant,'* she said under her breath, then dried herself with the cloth, shivering.

From under the bed Lib pulled out the chamber pot, which was clean. 'Did you use this at all, child?'

Anna nodded. 'Sister gave it to Kitty to empty.'

What was in it? Lib should have asked, but found she couldn't.

Anna pulled her nightdress back up over her shoulders. She wet the small cloth, then reached down under the linen to wash one leg modestly as she balanced on the other, holding the dresser to steady herself. The shimmy, drawers, dress and stockings she put on were all yesterday's.

Lib usually insisted on a daily change, but she felt she couldn't in a family as poor as this one. She draped the sheets and blanket over the footboard to air before she began her examination of the girl.

> *Tuesday, August 9, 5:23 a.m.*
> *Water taken: 1 tsp.*
> *Pulse: 95 beats per minute.*
> *Lungs: 16 respirations per minute.*
> *Temperature: cool.*

Although temperature was guesswork, really, depending on whether the nurse's fingers happened to be warmer or colder than the patient's armpit.

'Put out your tongue, please.' By training Lib always noted the condition of the tongue, though she'd have been hard pressed to tell what it said about the subject's health. Anna's was red, with an odd flatness at the back instead of the usual tiny bumps.

When Lib put her stethoscope to Anna's navel, she heard a faint gurgling, though that could be attributed to the mixing of air and water; it didn't prove the presence of food. *Sounds in digestive cavity,* she wrote, *of uncertain origin.*

Today she'd have to ask Dr McBrearty about those swollen lower legs and hands. Lib supposed it could be argued that any symptoms arising from a limited diet were all to the good, because sooner or later, surely they'd provoke the girl to give up this grotesque charade. She made the bed again, tightening the sheets.

Later in the morning Lib took Anna out for another constitutional – only around the farmyard, because the skies were threatening. When Lib remarked on Anna's halting gait, the child said that was just how she walked. She sang hymns as she went like a stoical soldier.

'Do you like riddles?' Lib asked her when there came a break in the music.

'I don't know any.'

'Dear me.' Lib remembered the riddles of childhood more vividly than all the things she'd had to memorize in the schoolroom. 'What about this: *There's not a kingdom on the earth, but what I've travelled o'er and o'er, and whether it be day or night I neither am nor can be seen. What am I?*'

Anna looked mystified, so Lib repeated it.

'*I neither am nor can be seen,*' echoed the girl. 'Does that mean that I amn't – I don't exist – or I amn't seen?'

'The latter,' said Lib.

'Someone invisible,' said Anna, 'who travels all across the earth –'

'Or some*thing*,' Lib put in.

The child's frown lifted. 'The wind?'

'Very good. You're a quick study.'

'Another. Please.'

'Hm, let's see. *The land was white,*' Lib began,

> The seed was black,
> It'll take a good scholar
> To riddle me that.

'Paper, with ink on it!'

'Clever puss.'

'It was because of *scholar*.'

'You should go back to school,' Lib told her.

Anna looked away, towards a cow munching grass. 'I'm all right at home.'

'You're an intelligent girl.' The compliment came out more like an accusation.

Kitty finally brought in Lib's breakfast: two eggs and a cup of milk. This time, greed made Lib eat so fast, tiny fragments of shell crunched in her teeth. The eggs were gritty and reeked of peat; roasted in the ashes, no doubt.

How could the child bear not just the hunger, but the boredom?

A knock at the front door, shortly after ten. Lib heard a muffled conversation. Then Rosaleen O'Donnell tapped on the door of the bedroom and looked past the nurse. 'More guests for you, pet. Half a dozen of them, some of them come all the way from America.'

The child nodded, as if pleased for her mother's sake more than her own.

The big Irishwoman's sprightliness sickened Lib; she was like some chaperone at a debutante's first ball. 'I should have thought it obvious that such visits must be suspended, Mrs O'Donnell.'

'Why so?' The mother jerked her head over her shoulder towards the good room. 'These seem like decent people.'

'The watch requires conditions of regularity and calm for the full fortnight. Without any way of checking what visitors may have on them –'

The woman interrupted. 'What kind of what?'

'Well, food,' said Lib.

'Sure there's food in this house already without anyone shipping it all the way across the Atlantic.' Rosaleen O'Donnell let out a laugh. 'Besides, Anna doesn't want it; haven't you seen proof of that by now?'

Lib met the woman's pebble eyes. 'My job is not only to make sure that no one passes the child anything, but that nothing is hidden where she can find it later.'

'Whyever would they do that when they've come all this way to see the amazing little girl who *doesn't* eat?'

'Nonetheless.'

Mrs O'Donnell's lips set hard. 'Our guests are in the house already, so they are, and 'tis too late to turn them away without grave offence.'

At this point it occurred to Lib to slam the bedroom door and set her back against it.

The woman's pebble eyes held hers.

Lib decided to give in until she could speak to Dr McBrearty. *Lose a battle, win the war.*

She led Anna into the good room and took up her position right behind the child's chair.

The visitors were a gentleman from the western port of Limerick with his wife and in-laws and a mother and daughter of their acquaintance, visiting from the United States. The older American lady volunteered the information that the two of them were Spiritualists. 'We believe the dead speak to us.'

Anna nodded, matter-of-fact.

'Your case, my dear, strikes us as the most glorious proof of the power of the mind.' The lady leaned over to squeeze the child's fingers.

'No touching, please,' said Lib, and the visitor jerked back.

Rosaleen O'Donnell put her head in the door to offer them a cup of tea.

Lib was convinced the woman was provoking her. *No food*, she mouthed.

One of the gentlemen was interrogating Anna about the date of her last meal.

'April the seventh,' she told him.

'That was your eleventh birthday?'

'Yes, sir.'

'And how do you believe you've survived this long?'

Lib expected Anna to shrug or say she didn't know. Instead she murmured something that sounded like *mamma*.

'Speak up, little girl,' said the older Irishwoman.

'I live on manna from heaven,' said Anna. As simply as she might have said, *I live on my father's farm*.

Lib shut her eyes briefly so as not to roll them in disbelief.

'Manna from heaven,' the younger Spiritualist repeated to the elder. 'Fancy that.'

The visitors were pulling out presents now. From Boston, a toy called a thaumatrope; did Anna have anything like it?

'I haven't any toys,' she told them.

They liked that; the charming gravity of her tone. The Limerick gentleman showed her how to twist the disc's two strings, then twirl them, so the pictures on the two sides blurred into one.

'The bird's in the cage now,' marvelled Anna.

'Aha,' he cried, 'mere illusion.'

The disc slowed and stopped, so the empty cage was left on the back, and the bird on the front flew free.

After Kitty brought the tea in, the wife produced something even more curious: a walnut that popped open in Anna's hand to let out a crumpled ball that relaxed into a pair of exquisitely thin yellow gloves. 'Chicken skin,' said the lady, fondling them. 'All the rage when I was a child. Never made anywhere in the world but Limerick. I've kept this pair half a century without tearing them.'

Anna drew the gloves on, finger by fat finger; they were too long, but not by much.

'Bless you, my child, bless you.'

Once the tea was drunk, Lib made a pointed remark about Anna needing to rest.

'Would you say a little prayer with us first?' asked the lady who'd given her the gloves.

Anna looked to Lib, who felt she had to nod.

'*Infant Jesus, meek and mild*,' the girl began,

Look on me, a little child.
Pity mine and pity me,
Suffer me to come to Thee.

As they left, Lib listened to the coins clink into the money box.

Back in the narrow bedroom, they heard the bell chime in the kitchen and Anna dropped to the floor. (No wonder the child's shins were bruised.) The minutes ticked by while the prayers of the angelus filled the air. Like being locked up in a monastery, Lib thought.

'*Through the same Christ Our Lord, Amen.*' Anna got up and gripped the back of the chair.

'Dizzy?' asked Lib.

Anna shook her head and readjusted her shawl.

'How often must you all do this?'

'At noon, only,' said the child. ' 'Twould be better to say it at six in the morning and in the evening as well, but Mammy and Dadda and Kitty are too busy.'

After her shift Lib picked her way along the dirty lane, which was potholed with ovals of blue sky; last night's rain. She was coming to the conclusion that without a fellow nurse working to Lib's own high standards – Miss Nightingale's own standards – the whole watch was flawed. For lack of due vigilance over a crafty child, all this trouble and expense might go to waste.

And yet Lib had seen no real evidence of craftiness in the girl yet. Except for the one vast lie, of course: the claim of living without food.

She asked for directions to Dr McBrearty's.

His house was a substantial one at the end of a lane, some way out on the Athlone Road. A maid as decrepit as her master showed Lib into the study. McBrearty whipped off his octagonal glasses as he stood up.

Vanity? she wondered. Did he fancy he looked younger without them?

'Good afternoon, Mrs Wright. How are you?'

Irked, Lib thought of saying. *Frustrated. Thwarted on all sides.*

'Anything of an urgent nature to report?' he asked as they sat.

'Urgent? Not exactly.'

'No hint of fraud, then?'

'No positive evidence,' Lib corrected him. 'But I thought you might have visited your patient to see for yourself.'

His sunken cheeks flushed. 'Oh I assure you, little Anna's on my mind at all hours. In fact, I'm so very concerned for the watch that I've thought it best to absent myself so it can't be insinuated afterwards that I've exerted any influence over your findings.'

Lib let out a small sigh. McBrearty still seemed to be assuming that the little girl would be proved a modern-day miracle. 'I'm concerned that Anna's temperature seems low, especially in her extremities.'

'Interesting.' McBrearty rubbed his chin

'Her skin's not good,' Lib went on, 'nor her nails, nor her hair.' This sounded like petty stuff from a magazine of beauty. 'And there's a downy fuzz growing all over her. But what worries me most is the swelling in her legs – her face and hands, too, but the lower legs are the worst. She's resorted to wearing her brother's old boots.'

'Mm, yes, Anna's been dropsical for some time. Puzzling. However, she doesn't complain of pain.'

'Well. She doesn't complain at all.'

The doctor nodded as if that reassured him. 'Digitalis is a proven remedy for fluid retention, but of course she won't take anything by mouth. One might resort to a dry diet –'

'Limit her liquids even further?' Lib's voice shot upwards. 'She has only a few spoonfuls of water a day as it is.'

Dr McBrearty plucked at his side whiskers. 'I could reduce her legs mechanically, I suppose.'

Bleeding, did he mean? Leeching? Lib wished she hadn't said a word to this antediluvian.

'But that has its own risks. No, no, on the whole, safer to watch and wait.'

Lib was still uneasy. Then again, if Anna was imperilling her own health, whose fault was it but her own? Or the fault of whoever was putting her up to this, Lib supposed.

'She doesn't look like a child who hasn't eaten in four months, does she?' the doctor asked.

'Far from it,' said Lib.

'My sense of it exactly! A wonderful anomaly.'

The old man had misunderstood her. He was wilfully blind to the obvious conclusion: the child was getting fed somehow. 'Doctor, if Anna were really taking no nourishment at all, don't you think she'd be prostrated by now? Of course you must have seen many famished patients during the potato blight, far more than I,' Lib added as a sop to his expertise.

McBrearty shook his head. 'As it happens, I was still in Gloucestershire then. I inherited this estate only five years ago and couldn't rent it out, so I thought I'd return and practice here.' He rose to his feet as if to say their interview was over.

'Also,' she went on in a rush, 'I can't say I have the utmost confidence in my fellow nurse. It will be no easy task to maintain complete alertness during night shifts in particular.'

'But Sister Michael should be an old hand at that,' said McBrearty. 'She nursed at the Charitable Infirmary in Dublin for twelve years.'

Oh. Why had nobody thought to tell Lib this?

'And at the House of Mercy, they rise for night office at midnight, I believe, and again for lauds at dawn.'

'I see,' said Lib, mortified. 'Well. The real problem is that the conditions at the cabin are most unscientific. I have no way to weigh the child, and there are no lamps to provide adequate light. Anna's room can easily be accessed from the kitchen, so anyone might go in when I take her out walking. Without your authority, Mrs O'Donnell won't even let me shut the door to oglers, which makes it impossible to watch the child rigorously enough. Could I have it in your hand that there are to be no visitors admitted?'

'Quite, yes.' McBrearty wiped his pen on a cloth and took up a fresh page. He fumbled in his breast pocket.

'The mother may resist turning away the mob, of course, on account of the loss of money.'

The old man blinked his rheumy eyes and kept digging in his pocket. 'Oh, but the donations all go into the poor box that Mr Thaddeus gave the O'Donnells. You don't understand these people if you think they'd keep a farthing.'

Lib's mouth set. 'Are you by any chance looking for your spectacles?' She pointed to where they lay among his papers.

'Ah, very good.' He jammed the side arms over his ears and began to write. 'How do you find Anna otherwise, may I ask?'

Otherwise? 'In spirits, you mean?'

'In, well, in character, I suppose.'

Lib was at a loss. A nice girl. But a cheat of the deepest dye. Anna had to be. Didn't she? 'Generally calm,' she said instead. 'What Miss Nightingale used to describe as an accumulative temperament, the kind that gathers in impressions gradually.'

McBrearty brightened up at the name, so much so that Lib wished she hadn't used it. He signed the note and held it out.

'Could you have it sent over to the O'Donnells', please, to put a stop to these visits this very afternoon?'

'Oh certainly.' He tugged off his glasses again, folding them in half with tremulous fingers. 'Fascinating letter in the latest *Telegraph*, by the by.' McBrearty stirred the papers on his desk without finding what he was looking for. 'It mentions a number of previous cases of "fasting girls" who've lived without food – have been said to do so, at least,' he corrected himself, 'in Britain and abroad over the centuries.'

Really? Lib had never heard of the phenomenon.

'The writer suggests that they might possibly have been, ah – well, not to put too fine a point on it – reabsorbing, subsisting on their own menses.'

What a revolting theory. Besides, this child was only eleven. 'In my view, Anna is a long way from being pubescent.'

'Mm, true.' McBrearty looked dashed. Then the corners of his mouth turned up. 'To think I might have stayed in England,' he murmured, 'and never had the luck to encounter such a case!' ∎

THE MOUNTAIN ROAD

William Wall

James Casey drove off the top of Rally Pier. His two daughters were on the back seat. The tide here falls out through the islands and away west. It runs at a knot, sometimes a knot and a half at springs. Listen and you will hear it in the stones. This is the song of lonely places. The car moved a little sideways as it sank. And afterwards great gulps of air escaped but made no sound. I know these things, not because I saw them but because they must have happened. The sky is settling over Rally and the hills. It is the colour of limestone, a great cap on the country. Ten miles out the sky is blue.

I heard it on local radio, suicide at Rally Pier. I knew who it was.

You cannot see the pier from my house. I got up and put my jeans and jumper on and climbed the hill behind the house, through heather and stone, to where I could look down. Bees sang in the air. Watery sunshine filtered through thin clouds. When I turned after ten minutes of climbing, the whole bay lay before me, the islands in their pools of stillness, the headlands like crude fingers, boats pair-trawling a mile or more apart but connected forever by cables attached to the wings of a giant net. James was on the boats once. He it was who explained all that to me. I saw the police tape on the pier head, a tiny yellowness that was not there before. If he left a note, what did it say? Suddenly the song came into my head. Donal Óg. Even as the first words came I knew what it meant for me. You took the east from me and you took the west from me and great is my fear that you took God from me.

When the song was finished with me I walked back down home. I was accustomed to think of it like that – not that I stopped singing but that the song was finished with me. I made up the bed with fresh sheets and put the soiled ones in the washing machine. I washed out the floor of the bathroom. Why do we do these things when we are bereft? Then I had a shower and put on dark clothes. I got out the bicycle and pumped up the leaking tyre. My father had shown me how to mend punctures but I could not remember now. I still have the same puncture repair kit, a tin box, but now I keep hash in it.

Then I wheeled the bicycle down to the gate and onto the road and faced the hill to the house where the dead girls lay.

They closed the door against me when they saw me turn the bend. Cousins make these decisions, but I leaned my bicycle against the wall and knocked and then they had to let me in. Perhaps it was inevitable anyway. People around here do not shut their neighbours out. They showed me into the front room where the two girls lay in open coffins. Three older women sat by them. I did not recognise them. Aunts, most probably. They had their beads in their hands. I did not bless myself. I go to neither church nor chapel and they all know it. I stood for a long time looking down on the faces. When old people go, death eases their pain and their faces relax into a shapeless wax model of someone very like them. People say they look happy, but mostly they look plastic. But when a child dies it is the perpetuation of a certain model of perfect beauty. People would say the girls looked like angels. There was no trace of the sea on them, no sign of the panic and fear that bubbled through the ground-up sleeping tablets that their father had fed them for breakfast yesterday morning. According to local radio. His own prescription. He had not been sleeping for months.

When I stopped looking I shook hands with each of the aunts.

Nobody said anything. I went out of the room and found the cousins waiting in the corridor. I asked for Helen and was told she was lying down. The doctor was calling regularly all day. She was on tablets for her nerves. She was very low. I was about to ask them to pass on my sympathy when a door opened upstairs. It was Helen herself. She called to know who was there. It's your neighbour, one of the cousins said. She could not bring herself to name me.

Helen came unsteadily down the stairs.

Her hair was flat and moist. She was wearing the kind of clothes she might have gone to Mass in, a formal blouse and a straight grey skirt, but she had no tights on. Her bare feet looked vulnerable and childish. She stepped deliberately, stretching so that at each tread of the stairs she stood on the ball of her foot like a dancer. She came down like someone in a trance. I think we all wondered if she knew who she was coming down for. And if she did, what was she going to say.

Cáit, she said, is it yourself? Thank you for coming.

Her eyes were flat, too. There was no light in them.

I'm sorry for your trouble, I said, taking her hand. I held the hand tightly as if the pressure could convey something in itself.

Helen shook her head.

Why did he do it? she said. Even if he went himself. But the girls . . .

Helen, will I make you a cup of tea?

One of the cousins said that. She was by Helen's side now, she would like to take her arm and lead her into the kitchen. They did not want her going into the front room and starting the wailing and the cursing all over again. Jesus, Mary and Joseph, it would terrify you to hear the things she said. And here she was now talking to Cáit Deane like nothing had happened at all.

There was cake and several kinds of bread and honey and tea and coffee and a bottle of the hard stuff and stout and beer. The house was provided against a famine. They'd need it all by and by. This is the way things go at funerals.

He always spoke well of you, Helen said.

We were childhood sweethearts, I said.

He always said you should have trained professionally. He said you had a great voice.

I shrugged. I heard this kind of thing from time to time.

He said it was pity what happened to you.

I felt my shoulders straighten. I was fond of him, I said, everybody was.

He said you had terrible bitterness in you.

I moved towards the door but there was a cousin in the way. Excuse me, I said. The cousin did not move. She had her arms folded. She was smiling.

He said you were your own worst enemy.

I turned on her. Well he was wrong there, I said. I have plenty of enemies.

Helen Casey closed her eyes. The only thing my husband was wrong about was that he took my two beautiful daughters with him. If he went on his own nobody would have a word to say against him. But now he cut himself off from everything. Even our prayers. If that man is burning in Hell, it's all the same to me. I hope he is. He'll never see my girls again for they're not in Hell. And the time will come when you'll join him and no one will be sorry for that either.

One of the cousins crossed herself and muttered under her breath. Jesus, Mary and Joseph.

The doorkeeper unfolded her arms suddenly and stepped aside. I opened the door. I was taken by surprise to find the priest outside preparing to knock.

Oh, he said.

Excuse me, Father.

I pushed past him. I noticed that the tyre was sinking again; it would need pumping but I could not do it here. I turned it to face away from the house. People say I'm cold. A cold-hearted bitch, some of them say. They say such things. The priest was watching me. He was smiling. The new man in the parish, most likely he did not know who I was. They'd fill him in on the details in the front room with the two dead girls and the old women with their beads. The cousins would know everything. It was how crows always knew there was bread out. First came a single bird, a scout. There was always one. Then they gather. Before long they're fighting each other over crusts. You can knock fun out of watching them and their comical battles in the backyard. But the minute you put the bread out, one of them turns up to check it out and the others follow soon enough. If you dropped dead on your own lawn they'd be down for your eyes.

I swung into my bicycle and launched myself down the tarmac drive and out onto the road and I turned for the hill down home but that was not where I was going.

I met the car at the place where the road was falling into the valley. There was no question of slipping past. I braked hard and dragged my foot along the road. By the time I stopped I was by the driver's door and there was a drop of a hundred feet on my left-hand side. He rolled the window down. It was James's brother Johnny.

You'd think the council would shore that up, he said.

The crows are gathering.

He nodded.

The priest was at the door.

He nodded again. He looked at me silently for a moment, then he said, He could have asked for help, Cáit. You'd have helped him, wouldn't you? I would any day. All he had to do was ask.

Johnny, I said, you know very well I was the last one he'd turn to. And the last one who could help him. And anyway, there is no help.

You could but you would not.

No, I said, I just could not. You know that very well.

Do you know what, Cáit Deane?

I probably do, Johnny.

He looked at me, frustrated. You were always the same. You're too sharp for around here.

I shrugged.

My brother James, he said, you destroyed him.

He destroyed himself. I didn't drive him down to the pier.

Why did he do it if not for you? You took him. You took him and you wouldn't keep him and then you left him. Why else would he do it?

I got my foot on the pedal again and faced down the hill.

Spite, I said. He was always spiteful, like a spoiled child.

I launched myself forward and went clear of the car. In a moment I was past the subsiding section. Fuchsia speckled the roadsides with their first bloody skirts. In the valley the last of the whitethorn blossom. The river at the very bottom gleaming like concrete in a field of bog iris. And ahead was the bay and its islands and the vast intolerant ocean.

I chained the bicycle to the stop sign outside the funeral home. The street was a long one that ran into a steep hill; the funeral home, the graveyard and the church were all at the top of the hill so that the dead could look down on the town, and the townspeople when they looked up from the pavement saw death looming like a public monument to their future. People joked that it was the only town in Ireland where you had to climb up to your grave. To make matters worse, the funeral home was owned by the Hill family. There were several Hills in the parish and naturally the funeral home was called the Hilton. They say that the only people making money out of the economic crash were accountants and funeral directors. Even the bankrupt had to be buried by somebody. At the door in a plastic frame was a poster with a picture of an anorexic bonsai plant and the words: OUR PROMISE TO YOU, PHONE ANYTIME, DAY OR NIGHT, YOU WILL NEVER GET AN ANSWERING MACHINE.

Funeral homes are always cold. There were pine benches in lines like a church. They had been varnished recently and there was that heady smell. It reminded me of my father's boat, the wheelhouse brightwork newly touched up. It was the smell of childhood.

James Casey lay in a plain wooden box at the top of the room. I could see immediately that the brass handles were fake. Someone had examined a funeral menu and ticked cheap. I went to look down on him. I thought I had nothing to say but when I was standing there I had plenty.

You stupid bastard, I said, you stupid murdering fucking bastard.

There was more like that. I surprised myself at the flow of anger, the dam-burst of fury. After a time I stopped because I was afraid I was going to attack the corpse. And then I thought I might have been shouting. No one came; perhaps funeral directors and their secretaries are used to angry mourners. I stepped back and found my calf touching a bench. I sat down.

They'll all blame me, I told him. They already blame me.

Then I cried.

James Casey looked tranquil and unperturbed. In real life he was never like that. After a time I got up. I looked down at him. His eyes were stitched closed because when he was pulled from the sodden car of course they were open. They are not very expert in our part of the world; I could see the stitches here and there. The funeral director knows from experience that the eyes of dead people do not express emotion but he knows that his clients would see fear in them. Nobody wants to look a dead man in the eye. It's bad for business.

Fuck you, I said.

I turned on my heel and walked out. A tiny sigh escaped when I closed the door, like the seal opening on an airtight jar. My bicycle lay on the ground in its chains. They knifed the tyres while I was with James. I was not going to give them the satisfaction of watching me wheel it down the street. I was going to leave it where I found it. Do not slouch, my mother used to say, stand up straight, put your shoulders back. But I slouched just the same. How many years since I first loved James Casey? I pulled my shoulders back but I kept my eyes on the ground. The thought that I had done something unforgivable was always there in the dark. Things come back in the long run, the way lost things are revealed by the lowest tides: old shipwrecks, old pots, the ruined moorings that once held steadfastly to trawlers or pleasure boats. There are no secrets around here. ∎

THROUGH THE NIGHT

Siobhán Mannion

O n the floor of the hotel corridor they sit, either side of a bottle of wine, the world dark beyond a huge sloped window, their bodies reflected, slumped against an inner wall. In easy silence, they sip from their glasses, knowing that in a few short hours they will both fly home. She slides off her shoes, stretches her legs, smooths her new skirt over her thighs. His left foot tips against her right. She holds her breath against this pleasure; a flash of lightning brings her round.

'Wow, that's some storm,' she says.

'Well, I guess that's the end of that,' he says, a sudden energy in his voice. 'We won't see anything tonight.'

They have stayed up late to watch the space station, another spacecraft moving in to dock. She heard some of the delegates mention it at breakfast, later searched for details online. A crack of thunder vibrates beneath them, rain slashing the floor-to-ceiling glass wall. In the dim night-time lighting of the corridor, he makes a move to go.

'I enjoyed your talk this morning,' she says, a little louder now.

'Did you really?' he says, relaxing back down. 'Which part?'

'Well . . .' All she had really noticed were his hands moving, how he held himself at the podium. He brings his knees to his chest.

She takes another mouthful of wine. Her weekend has been spent watching all of them, barely registering their words, concentrating on time passing, one half-hour at a time. When his turn came, she could picture him in his studio, throwing colours at a wall.

'I enjoyed yours too,' he says, rescuing her. 'Especially that last piece you read, about your husband.'

She hands him back the bottle, observes the thrashing of the world outside. Her hotel room waits twelve floors away, graced with its mountain view. Three days she has dressed and undressed there, curtains open, vast sky bearing down; the invitation to come here the first she has accepted in almost a year. On this, the ground floor, she senses the depth of the valley, the town that pulls away from this enormous building on a mountainside.

A cleaner approaches, moving quickly, pushing her cart straight ahead. They make their bodies small. The girl gives no reaction, her soft shoes squeaking over the hard floor. This gathering has brought dozens of them: artists, composers, writers from around the globe. They are the last two, long since kicked out of the function room, all the others gone to bed.

'You remind me of someone,' he says, close to her ear. She notices the threads of darker linen running down the front of his shirt, the slow movement of his chest as he breathes. 'Are you drunk?' he asks.

'Of course not. No, no, no.'

She has put the emphasis on all the right syllables, made comedy out of nothing at all. And it comes, the laughter that obliterates the need to make any more talk for a while. They sit, the moment expanding, united by the storm.

'Tell me about your marriage,' he says, after a while.

'What's to tell? He died. I got old.'

When she hears it, she feels the truth of it. When she closes her eyes, he squeezes her hand. She welcomes the momentary pressure from his fingers, soft and unexpectedly warm.

'Do you like living in the city?' he asks. 'Do you usually work from home?'

They ask questions of each other; new pieces of information standing in for all the years until now. He smells of soap and alcohol.

At registration she saw him see her, knew he would make her acquaintance, seek her out from then on.

'What's the most beautiful thing you own?'

She considers this, and smiles. 'Nothing I could show you,' she replies. 'How did your last day go?'

'Good,' he says, finishing his wine.

Strange that it's the same day, she thinks, lived inside different lives. The storm has eased off, quietened down, the wind driving raindrops across the window. She puts both hands to the floor, which has started to tip underneath her.

'I shouldn't have come,' she says.

'Of course you should.' They look carefully into each other's eyes. 'For all those people hanging on your every word.' He smiles.

'Ha,' she says, 'you're sweet,' letting herself lean in. In the dark glass, her head has found his shoulder. She releases an audible breath, reminds herself that he likes men, allows a little more weight to fall. In her room, they could be drinking tea with capsules of milk, tearing sachets of sugar, biting into individually foil-wrapped biscuits.

Her back slips an inch down the wall. When she rights herself, he is tapping on his phone. He has captured their reflection: two bodies elongated under glass.

'I didn't come here to be beamed around the place,' she says.

'It's hardly that,' he says, and laughs. 'And, anyway, it's not as if this is what we actually look like.' His thumb continues its dance over the screen. 'I went up onto the roof today. Here, look at this. It would make a great backdrop for something, don't you think?'

She squints at the brightness until the colours coalesce into an image: sky, mountains, a distant cluster of low buildings. Her head feels heavy, peering down into the phone. They are joined at the hip now, the wine bottle no longer between them. She holds onto her heartbeat, under the breast, pounding the bone.

'Hey!' he says, leaping to the window, the empty bottle sent careering along the floor. And she wonders whether they will see the space station after all. His back arches, the fingers of one hand spreading out against the glass. 'Must have been a trick of the light,' he says, quietly, to himself.

'Oh, well,' she says mildly, as if distracting a child. He doesn't react. 'You know, up there, they make night by pulling the shutters down.'

'Who?'

'The people living in space.' He turns to look at her. 'And they spend hours and hours of every day working out.' She joins him at the window. 'Because of gravity. The body breaks down with nothing to push against.' He nods, absently, taking a small step back. 'You okay? You don't seem yourself,' she says.

'I'm fine. Just tired, that's all,' he says.

'And drunk,' she laughs. He frowns. She hasn't thought about her words, about how meaning is made from sounds; she is aware, all at once, of the risk in conversation, every second of it improvised.

'I think it's time to call it a night,' he says, glancing at his watch.

She puts her forehead against the window, tilting back to accommodate its angle. 'Goodnight,' she says, without making eye contact.

'Goodnight,' he says. She senses his hesitation, then listens as he leaves, waiting until there is nothing except the sounds of her own breath. The harsh lighting of the deserted function room reveals its shabbiness when she passes, resting a hand on the door frame to steady herself. In the far corner, one of the giant display boards has toppled, and lies abandoned, face down. She walks the hotel's long corridors, heels in hand, over concrete, carpet and tile. The lift shudders as it ascends.

Twelve flights later, she sits on the huge bed, peels off her clothes: the new skirt, the pale silk blouse. For a long time she works her thumb against the clasp of her thin silver necklace, until the skin is dented and sore. Her phone has filled with messages, and she retrieves them, finger swiping the tiny screen: words typed, voices recorded, a video of her brother's children, laughing, on swings.

An image opens from an email sent only a few minutes before: two bodies in the dark, far away, huddled tight. 'look how small we are', reads the caption, all in lower case. She looks at it closely, zooming in and then out, staring at it long enough for it to dissolve into nothing more than shapes. In the bathroom, she wrestles with the splashy tap, pours a glass of water and gulps at it, her swallowing at odds with her breathing. The person in the mirror watches her, slightly swollen, slightly blurred. A little closer and she is even blurrier, this 44-year-old woman blinking at her, slack-jawed.

For almost two weeks, she lay wound around him, as much as the wires and the tubes would allow: her body curled up on a wide plastic chair, her head resting on her arms reaching out. One night, she took his left hand and slowly began to examine the length of each nail. Until the room was bleached in sudden light – everything quiet, everything noise – and filled with people working, signalling for her to get out of their way.

She pushes her head out the narrow window, sucks at the clean air, rotates herself to better see the stars. Up there, the skies clearing, it would be possible to make out one bright light gaining on another, the two of them hurtling side by side. A stinging breeze comes at her, fresh against the clammy heat of her skin. There is still time, she thinks. And then she's heading down the hall, in towelling robe and stockinged feet; counting down towards the relevant number, fully sure that he will open his door.

But, at a turn, she is sent sideways, stumbles, finds herself kneeling on the carpeted floor. A hotel worker drops a pile of towels, and rushes forward, a soft 'oh' escaping from her. It is the girl from downstairs, who meets her gaze, and then averts her eyes to give her time to pick herself up. For a brief moment, she gets tangled in the dressing gown's cord. Saliva starts to fill her mouth, her stomach lurching towards her throat. Eventually, she brings herself to standing, one hand pressed against the wall. With the girl at her side, she makes it back to her room.

On the bed, she lies wide-eyed, waiting to drop anchor, to sink into the unconscious part of her life. The soft mattress gives underneath her; she will wake to stiff bones, a sore neck. Carefully, she closes the robe over herself, bunching the thick cloth at her chest. The room spins hard. In the window, she concentrates on what surrounds her: the clean surfaces without trace of permanent life; the low lamplight doubled in the glass.

The girl is illuminated, crouching at the minibar, reaching in to pull something out. A bottle cap is untwisted, an open drink brought to the bedside table, a zing of lemons released into the air as the light clicks off. Swiftly, the girl draws the curtains, before circling back around the bed in the dark. She can track her by her breathing. She moves near enough for them to touch, if she put her hand out. ∎

OUR DAY WILL COME

LOYALIST, REPUBLICAN

Stephen Dock

Belfast, September 2012. Loyalists celebrate the centennial of the Ulster Covenant.

Belfast, April 2014. Republicans gather to listen to a speech in Ardoyne.

Derry, January 2015. A view of Creggan, a republican neighbourhood.

Belfast, July 2014. The bonfire for the Eleventh Night, a loyalist celebration of the Battle of the Boyne (1690).

Belfast, July 2014. A loyalist enclave in Tiger's Bay.

Belfast, April 2014. Republicans commemorate the Easter Rising at Milltown Cemetery.

Belfast, April 2014. Ardoyne, a working-class and mainly Catholic district.

Belfast, July 2014. Sandy Row, a loyalist neighbourhood.

Belfast, July 2014. A loyalist community near Botanic railway station.

Belfast, April 2014. Republican commemorations at Milltown Cemetery.

Same magazine, different format

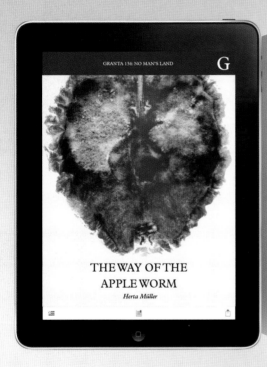

New app out now

GRANTA.COM

GRANTA

THE MAGAZINE OF NEW WRITING

PRINT SUBSCRIPTION REPLY FORM FOR US, CANADA
AND LATIN AMERICA (includes digital and app access).
For digital-only subscriptions, please visit granta.com/subscriptions.

GUARANTEE: If I am ever dissatisfied with my *Granta* subscription, I will simply notify you, and you will send me a complete refund or credit my credit card, as applicable, for all un-mailed issues.

YOUR DETAILS

TITLE ....
NAME ....
ADDRESS ....
....
CITY.. STATE ....
ZIP CODE ....COUNTRY................................
EMAIL ....

☐ Please check this box if you do not wish to receive special offers from *Granta*
☐ Please check this box if you do not wish to receive offers from organisations selected by *Granta*

PAYMENT DETAILS

1 year subscription: ☐ US: $48 ☐ Canada: $56 ☐ Latin America: $68

3 year subscription: ☐ US: $120 ☐ Canada: $144 ☐ Latin America: $180

Enclosed is my check for $ _____ made payable to *Granta*.

Please charge my: ☐ Visa ☐ MasterCard ☐ Amex

Card No. ☐☐☐☐☐☐☐☐☐☐☐☐☐☐☐☐

Expiration date ☐☐ / ☐☐

Security Code ☐☐☐☐☐

SIGNATURE .... DATE ....

Please mail this order form with your payment instructions to:

Granta Publications
PO Box 359
Congers, NY 10920-0359

Or call 845-267-3031
Or visit GRANTA.COM/SUBSCRIPTIONS for details

Source code: BUS134PM

KIDDIO AT THE WEDDING

Mary O'Donoghue

Kiddio was between shoe sizes when we went to my cousin's wedding in a superannuated church that smelled of cooked dust. All day he tottered like a sandpiper to cope with his Pumas' constriction. Before we lit out for the journey he walloped my hand away when I tried to slacken his laces, and the sharp report rustled up tears. They brimmed so quickly I had to tilt my head far back.

Not for the pain, no, I was thinking how much more drastic all this would be without him. For he had stood on a chair and zipped my dress to where it needed to be, and touched my hair, which there was no call for at all. I let him spritz gardenia in my elbow crooks and behind my ears. Soon we were all set. It was August then, and so hushed a morning it was hard to believe the tree crickets had played saws for hours last night.

We were only together, he and I, because I had ducked into the church for a pee back in June. It was the longest day of the year, and everything crept like molasses. The church was the biggest in town, with a back end as dour as a storage facility and the frontage made beautiful by rose of Sharon and a string of genial gargoyles. I hadn't been inside since I didn't know how long. Beeswaxed corridors and a poster from Isaiah, *Behold, I am doing a new thing!* I wondered the prophet didn't trim to a goatee and sign up for OkCupid.

When I walked back up the stairs twenty-five or so people had materialized against the lobby wainscotting. Their heads were slung low and they looked woebegone, especially the older in their number. There were intimations of beautiful bones and good looks in the younger ones. The overall picture gripped me, the collective sangfroid, the clothes all cut from the same rain cloud. I didn't see the two or three kids beaded among them.

Then, from the cockpits of Nissans and Subarus, came the wives of southern burghers, bringers of food on oblong plastic platters. They unfolded tables and snapped out plastic floral tablecloths. They billowed thermal waves of kindness and solicitude. My mother had been one of their reservists until she deserted in favour of the Northeast.

Some of them knew me from old. We regarded one another with the truculence of friends who had gone on to better things and didn't want reminding of the ungainly days.

They asked after my mother's welfare. I said she was much better, thanks, after a bout of midepigastric discomfort. *Her words not mine*, I told them, and I syllabized the thing out, *mid-epi, you get the rest.* They asked me to relay their good wishes and prayers. They said how just lovely it was I moved back to town after all this time. I was weakened in the blast of tuberose and goodwill, and it etherized me enough to stick around and help lay the tables.

The ringleader said the group standing against the wainscotting were *misfortunate people from the very worst place on earth.* They were being prepared for International Friendship Alliances while their refugee status was being ratified. Perhaps would I give some consideration to being an international friend? And I said yes. Not glibly so as to get out the door, nor was it dazzlement from the good deeds flaring round me like Friday-night lights. I said yes because I was asked. The ringleader smiled so approvingly I felt bashful and delighted and confused all in one hot mess. She said I could continue to help with disbursing shoes and clothes.

The misfortunates of the earth moved warily along the trestle tables, giving each platter some long scrutiny. They eschewed the rolled meats, the pepper jack cheese, the pickles and those pimento-stuffed olives I had never gone for because they looked like eyes with gangrene. They settled on the carrot sticks, celery, apple rings and isosceles bits of pita. They assembled modest little plates. Who knew how quietly twenty-five people could eat the crunchiest food? That's when I noticed the kids. They took slices of everything going. They sat on the carpet and tried each item. Anything repellant they slid through the gaps under their knees.

In a side room I helped another doyenne fuse sneakers to their feet. *Five years old, ballpark*, she said of the little boy who extended his socked feet to her, *No English and no name, and all the way here from one of the most terrible places on earth.* She plucked Pumas from a bushel of donations. *These people have seen the most unimaginable things.* Her voice stopped on a precipice. She turned the sneakers' green suede over and again, she inspected the soles for wear. She had a fraught place inside her that itched to see the terrible and unimaginable things for herself. She probably watched those YouTubes people were supposed to take down in the immediate aftermath of atrocity. She was the kind of person who knew herself for a good woman, but maintained a healthy vigilance all the same for the bad stuff there was out there.

My son lost an arm trying to help people like this, she said. She pronounced the damage by chopping her hand against her upper arm where the flesh was paler and going pendulous. I could only look at her eyes when they were looking down and away. She got the Pumas on the boy's feet and palped for his toes at the top. She gave him a *Well, look at you cutie*, then groaned herself to standing.

I had moved back to the town, the town where I was raised and schooled and churched, where I had been kissed and fingered and split with, the town I fled in a small U-Haul for a degree in computer science. I moved back from a West Coast job, from hunching in a carrel solving online banking snafus and testing encryption, from calls from people who could not see their salary deposited to their account, *Was the system down, what the hell was going on?* from watching the monthly amounts, credit, insurance, utilities, leaving their accounts. It was always surprising in its measly regularity. I had been doing this work for fifteen years.

I returned to be nearer my parents. They claimed infirmity every so often, plus they missed me like hell, my father said, his voice fracking at the end of phone calls, *like heh-ull.* They were in their forties when I was born, and they were morose alongside the lively ball-playing parents of my school friends. Much later, I gauged those same parents, in bell-bottom pants and blouse tails tied in bunches, were in and out of one another's houses for sex. There was a pinkness to their skin back then that wasn't entirely owing to the humidity.

My parents had dry indoor complexions and the faces of studious monks. When they finally took me on a beach holiday I was almost too old to enjoy it. Over and over I smacked into Gulf shore waves on a bodyboard printed with flamingos, but they never left their safe sand to join me. They taught middle school until retirement and then they gardened diligently.

They won me back home with a broken ankle, my mother's, incurred in heavy rain and a misjudged doorstep. The same week I had been counselling a colleague to spend money on one of those baths with door hatches and benches so she could stop worrying about her father taking a tumble. *You're so right,* she said, *you're too-too right.*

My parents gave me what they called the best bedroom. The window was filled with their crape myrtle, and it would bloom all over again, with lavender, by midsummer. My father shut and opened the blinds to enact the surprise it would be on those mornings. He put a hand to his chest and stepped back reverentially. He told me I wouldn't believe my eyes.

Slowly I came not to despise their apoplectic news presenters and their determination to shop for groceries in small moieties instead of one big weekly cart. I even got used to the woozy cerulean disinfectant cake they hung like an earring inside the toilet bowl. I realized I was fixing to be old, and there were worse ways of doing it than with people who ate candied yams late at night and sought one another's academic opinion in the matter of bowel movements. They had a new and brazen honesty in their advancing years. I heard my mother offer to insert the suppository if my father was having trouble. She even made a joke about needing a GPS. I let them at it, and they let me be.

To sit on the gray leather couch that yielded affably around me, to place a glass of sweet tea in the cupholder, to half-entertain my mother's account of one, no, *two* international professors she saw in the French bakery, all of it was clemency from the tetchy result-driven West Coast. She was liable to invite one of those professors home for dinner, then cluck for days about what to serve. And after her plan didn't pan out she would say he wasn't the stuff of a husband anyhow, not with a nomadic lifestyle like that, but a lovely man nonetheless.

I took a job in tech at the university library, and I moved into an apartment next door to the grocery store. My parents were injured by this but said not too much. The apartment was abjectly appointed on the corner of the second of three poured-concrete stories. The front window gave onto a distressing view of purple Christmas cabbages. Rain raised oily puddles in the grocery parking lot, peacock blue and burnt orange, and until well after midnight a corrosive smell of exhaust stole through the vents. The aisles of the grocery store were filled with college students. They dawdled in formation, and stared in perplexity at fresh produce like they were encountering obscene paintings. In the early mornings my toilet flushed with an ominous upskiddle. *Some bigger and better place will come up*, my father contributed.

The year turned over in its customary manner. Agreeable chilliness gave way to spring nights when the skies shook and snapped sheets of lightning. The Doppler hemorrhaged nearby tornadoes, said to be seen on the ground somewhere, never coming close. My parents watched television for acts of terror and old-house renovation. The next year was not all that different.

My parents were the ones to move on. There was something loudly embarrassing about it. It's considered the most terrible thing to outlive a child, but what about when fiendishly selfish parents outflank you and head for the doughty preppy life of the Northeast? I put this to them, with my hands spread as wide on the kitchen table as if I were pushing a car backwards.

My father remonstrated with me in full cool phlegm. Had I forgotten it was *always part of the plan*, did he not have roots in New England after all? The shipshape little house with the steep shingled roof would be mine when the time came, was that not a consideration? Snow would always slide off such a roof, and it wasn't so very difficult to manage five months of winter. *Hell, it was downright cosy, as long as you had enough logs and food.* He had stopped spreading one-syllable words across two for maximum emotive impact, the charlatan.

From up there they posted to Facebook every day. They pointed out some curious domestic or village feature, a kitchen hutch with handles made from big old playing marbles, a shop that sold fishing flies far too beautiful to be fishing flies. My mother tried to buy some for earrings. I told her that's what all the old teachers in New England did, they wore feather earrings down to their shoulders. She was patient in the circumstance.

They even secured a dog, a wire-haired terrier called Thoreau. He came with the name, they said, and they hadn't the heart to change it. Besides, he was a strong-willed little so-and-so, unlikely to accept rebaptism. In one photo he sat between them on a picnic blanket and flashed the yellow incisors of a usurper.

I agreed to make a visit once they had completely settled in. I was assured of my very own bedroom. I put a running shoe beneath a cushion and sat on it and jumped up quickly in instinctive preparation for an accident involving Thoreau. I swore never to walk past their old house again.

I collected my little friend for the first time on a Sunday morning, in the lobby of the retirement home where he and his refugee friends were being housed until their status was ratified. The air was briny with lunch preparations and too many people. The church women were there to effect punctilious introductions, to make sure each refugee was paired with the correct international friend or friends.

There were families in troikas and some pairs of students. Everyone looked a little reluctant or bashful, but the church women had no truck with that and ushered people together. Had everyone done their homework concerning suggested activities for friendship families? Good, then they would see us back here in three hours. My assigned little friend stood fully still even as I took him by the hand. A refugee woman shrank to the dusty pink wallpaper when a sincere young blond couple stepped forward enthusiastically to make their claim on her.

I hadn't done the homework, so we walked around the building to see what there was to be seen. Pale green grass frizz-permed to brown on the verges. We found a declivity where the ground dropped off to red-brick rubble. A massive wall of beautyberry confronted us when we turned the last corner, its knots of vivacious phlox strung on stems like cheap jewelry. The air conditioner for the retirement home was as big as a shed. We walked past its baleful drone, then out into the neighborhood. We walked slowly so we could see what was on people's lawns and in the shape-shifting darkness at the back of open garages.

After an hour of silence, I told him I was his friend, we were international friends, we might be friends forever. My voice reverberated strangely, as it had done in times I had not spoken to a soul for several days. He said not a word, he made not a sound. I showed him a picture of Thoreau. At that he laughed, maybe because the dog was wearing knitted bootees, or maybe at the enchantment of the creature's sudden appearance on the screen and how we could evaporate him with a swipe.

After toying with Thoreau in that manner he chased an orange cat down the sidewalk. I gave him a stick of Twix and brought him back early. We sat awhile in the lobby. He paid baffled attention to two electric wheelchairs moving soundlessly along the carpet and out the front door. Their riders were synchronized in snazzy straw boaters and college football shirts.

The following week I brought him to my apartment to make pizza. My neighbor the ancient ex-marine was on the balcony reading a new fat paperback. *Well what've we got here, then?* His face went lax with sentiment, *What's new, kiddio?* He returned to the thrills and spills of his book. He could not give a damn about the little boy's origin, which made me like him a moment, he who was the soul of lechery, he who averred there was *nothing but nothing to look at when the college girls depart in May, not one bit of skirt in all of skirtnation.* I thought to bring a margherita slice out to him, but then I thought the better of it.

I started to use Kiddio as a placeholder until his status got ratified. I was comforted to have a name to tack onto the end of sentences, statements, inquiries, even if I didn't get an answer. We watched a video of the cool guy who sang *Won't you say yes, don't you say no, make me feel good, kiddio.* I told him the singer's slim gyrations were like my uncle's who used to walk backwards out a door singing, always desperate to please people he was leaving after a half-hour visit.

We went to playgrounds, down by the river, paved with that stuff kids supposedly bounce off if they fall. Kiddio never climbed or swung high enough to fall. He mostly walked around the base and looked up at kids clambering and sliding and advancing hand over hand. We went for ice cream and frozen yoghurt. People smiled affectionately at us, *Well look at you two.* Whenever it seemed like he might be silent for the entire outing, I brought Thoreau into play.

My cousin's wedding took place at a tiny non-working Methodist chapel, followed by a hair-down at a country club. Nobody in the picture was Methodist. My cousin had somehow wrested the chapel from the heritage council for a day. She posted that she wanted a wedding with the illusion of a full congregation. She would *stuff it to the rafters*, she said, she would *pack it cheek to cheek*.

It was an hour's drive each way. Birthday parties were on the International Friendship Alliance's list of suggested activities, weddings were not, and certainly not anything that far out of town. I asked my church woman permission for a six-hour visit with my international friend. I said we planned to throw and fire and paint clay pots. I weighed that insider terms like *throw* and *fire* would be compelling to her, and indeed she flushed with earnestness. It was no problem, she told me, only I was to make sure the little guy didn't get worn out.

Many miles from the Methodist chapel I came to believe I was in the wedding cavalcade. Faces in the next lane were tense and grim. They wanted this marriage to work, pray God let him show up! My cousin had a history of failed mergers, but finally, in the lurid Caribbean sun, she had beached a whale of a man. He worked in the high echelons of finance. He was by all accounts the catch of the county, my mother said, and she was just too-too sorry that my father's arthritis prevented them from traveling. They wanted full reports, though, they insisted on photos. They hoped I had found a nice friend to escort me. In the back seat Kiddio crackled and compounded an empty Doritos bag.

They knew not one thing about him. I had squeaked out of July Fourth at theirs by inventing malware that ripped callously through the university computer system. I told my father I was working nights to restore things back to health. My mother told me I was a marvel, she was proud of me, I would surely get a promotion on account of my valor. That Fourth weekend Kiddio and I ate ziti and meatballs and watched the Muppets scamper through New York in search of stolen jewels. We listened to the low crunks of fireworks going off near the river.

If I sent photos of Kiddio they would wonder whether caramel was accurate-and-or-acceptable to describe his skin. From there they would wonder who he had traveled to this country with. They would plan a trip of indefinite length to spend time with me. They would make early dinner, let me choose the movie, boil and reboil the kettle for chamomile tea. Then they would begin questions they hoped would lead to the real heart of the matter.

I would lose the exquisite discretion of napping on a blanket in a park, of waking up next to Kiddio in the shadow of clouds about to spill their innards. The thought of having to tell them so disconcerted the speed needle that it hit ninety. In the mirror I saw my little friend fall asleep. You don't get to see it very often, that twinkling when someone's heavy eyes stop fighting and latch on to sleep.

The Methodist chapel was insolently hot and musty, and somebody nearby was drenched in Chanel. The doors opened and my cousin steered herself inside. During two weeks' holiday in France I took a *Train à Grande Vitesse* from Paris to Marseille, where Scottish people stood in the scathing sun all flabbergasted and elated to have arrived so soon. *Here already? Really?* That was my cousin's face. She got her bearings, though, and she walked tulled and grinning past us, as smoothly as if a little turbine were working between her feet. At the front of the chapel stood the impassive dark backcloth of her financier. The crowd simpered like pigeons at the moving strangeness of it all.

An antediluvian great-aunt turned around to glare at Kiddio. He had been dunting her seat with some regularity, Puma on polished wood. She fixed cold as a raptor on him. She didn't recognize me, but I remembered her and the cigarillos she smoked one edgy Christmas we visited her in the mountains. Her eyes retreated to their rheum. She turned just as the bride drew level with her man. She clasped her old hands into tree roots exposed after high river.

Within half an hour the ceremony had succeeded in hitching the couple. The great-aunt's hands applauded with an uncooperative knapping sound. A profoundly suntanned reveler released silver confetti at the door. Kiddio sped from my side to grab some. I watched him wet his index fingers and dab tiny petals from the blacktop.

The reception at the country club was small and bespoke. Immense single magnolia blooms floated in glass punchbowls and there were healthy tasteful snacks at the bar. Somebody ordered a sidecar, and a panel of experts homed in to discuss the intrinsic virtues of various bourbons. The invitees were by and large friends and colleagues, with a few pearl-strung ancients from higher branches of the tree. The atmosphere was easygoing. I accepted a drink from a good old boy who said I was always his favorite of the town cousins. I bought a Coke for Kiddio, I propped two straws in it like flowers. We walked around holding hands, and we pecked at little wooden snack bowls.

My cousin came and stood behind me when I was reaching for bread at dinner. She rested her hands on my shoulders. She had visited everyone in this beatific manner. The cuffs of her wedding dress were tight enough for weals, but she had a gorgeous manicure, pale pink waning to white crescents. I smelled the rosy waxiness of her lipstick as into my ear she said it was good to see me after so long, that she made sure to invite me because we were only two weeks apart in age after all, that she felt we each measured ourselves by the other's destiny, and did I not feel like that? I told her I had felt a disturbance in the force when she met her financier, so yes, we must be somehow conjoined. She told me I was as cynical as ever, but she loved it all the same and she always would. She told me to get out there and enjoy myself.

After dinner Kiddio delighted the younger women. They bent at the waist and stretched out their arms to him. They looked like British royals at hospitals for sick children. I steered him from their reach, I said he was extremely shy. To a person they all thought he was mine, some fiat of adoption or a prize from a handsome-mystery-father-unknown. Nobody had the temerity to ask. *Beautiful boy,* a woman said to me in the ladies' room mirror, *He'll be a stunner, you mind you remember I told you that!* A few minutes earlier and she would have heard me coaxing him to squeeze out the remaining number two, that last bit always so intractable. I pressed my hands to my cheeks and pushed my face in against my nose and mouth, breathing out in a slow building hiss. I heard the placid plop, I watched his face unclench from torment. We had our system, and it worked just fine.

When dancing time came around I let none of them take him for a twirl. I held him on my knees and relented only to carry him onto the parquet floor. He clasped his legs around my waist and I held his hands tight as a tango. He kicked my hips to make me go faster, he chortled at my troubles. I made it off the floor rickety and exhausted. I was nothing but a fool for him.

C lose to leaving, Kiddio wanted to go down to the dock on the lake behind the country club. The light was dropping to evening, mosquitoes were limbering their mouthparts, but he had to visit the little wooden pagoda. He latched to my wrist with both hands, dug his heels back and hauled. There was something so very winning about the gesture. Back at the wedding a woman had belabored a man onto the floor that way, towing and wheedling. He was the only unaccompanied male, outback-looking in loose linen, and she wound her way around him like cat briar.

Kiddio and I sat on a bench inside the pagoda. There were soft conciliatory creaks, wood to water's undertow. If he fell in I would jump straight after, I would plumb through water not cold so much as oily, and dark as a dirty wine bottle. I would drag him up by the shirt collar, I would cup my hand under his and swim with my free arm, I would lay him on the warm decking lumber. I would massage his chest and breathe into his mouth until he blurted out what portion of lake he had swallowed. The whole thing would take only minutes, a precise and perfect sliver of time to bind us together for the rest of our lives. One time my father came home from the dentist amused and huffed both. The dentist had told him the filling would last him for *the duration*. They must have blinked at one another like desperadoes, the surgery clock ticking down the appointment.

I let Kiddio extricate his feet from the Pumas and peel off his socks. His feet were solid wedges, no arch to speak of. I rolled his pants and hoiked them up beyond the knee. I let him walk to the edge of the dock, I let him stub the water with his toes.

If someone is hanging from a window ledge or the scruff of a cliff you are best not to grasp their hands, for they will slip through your fingers. But if they clamp you above your wrist, and you hold them that same way, then there is a better chance of not letting go. So it was I dandled Kiddio in the lake. First to the tops of his knees. My feet were planted stout and wide on the dock. Then I lowered him further, to his waist, where the water made incursions on his bared belly, then a little further down. The hair on his head was buzz cut to a dark gray downiness, and there was a smidge of sunburn on the tops of his ears. He made no sound. I wanted something to issue from him, some call like a bird or a forest animal. But in the silent dead weight of his body and the small tight circumference of his grip he needed me more than anything.

Who would call me to attention, who would yell some frenzied halt from the long porch where they were boozing out the end of the day? Who would be sober and sensible enough to figure a yell would startle me, so who all in the name of God would sneak up behind and calmly save the situation? The man in loose linen maybe, if he had not been brought captive to some storeroom behind the kitchen. The music from the wedding was now Frank and Nancy Sinatra, singing insinuations about how to go and spoil it all.

I wrung Kiddio's pants in the pagoda. He looked out on the lake, po-faced as an owl. Gnats began to drizzle in our direction.

On the drive back we turned in to a rest stop. I had to hustle Kiddio from the back seat, I had to hold an imagined penis in my hand and hiss so he'd know why we were there. He didn't want out, and he hit my hand for the second time that day.

The day's heat was hanging round in sultry leftovers. My dress bit the backs of my knees, and I worked to flap it free on the walk to the restrooms. I held Kiddio tight by me.

We slowed to watch a long-distance truck driver drop heavily from his cab. He doubled over to grip his ankles, big man, he did it five times. At each rep he stayed longer to brood. I wondered where he had come from and how far he had yet to go. His eyes were tapered, as though still fixed on a road in the full beat of sunlight.

I let Kiddio trot ahead of me. He wanted nothing of me and each time I drew within arm's reach he shot forward. His jeans were dyed dark from the lake. We got our toilet business done, and I indicated the vending machine for a treat. He stood in the machine's wistful fog of green light, studying every sweet thing the shelves held to eat and drink.

I walked ahead to the bench where we would sit. Kiddio collected the cans from the drop drawer. He made slow and cautious work of it, pushing on the hatch, peering in, taking the first can and setting it on the ground. When he had both Coke Zero and Mountain Dew in hand he walked to the bench with a delirious grin. The air parped and burped with tree frogs. For a moment they dropped into silence, then made a triumphant return to lewdness. Out on the highway asphalt was getting poured from a caravan of huge square vehicles. Alongside them men in yellow vests walked like bodyguards. Large round lights, as absurdly beautiful and tremulous as Chinese lanterns, lit the work. Above the trees the stars were indisposed. I opened the can Kiddio couldn't snick for himself, nothing but nothing but happiness metastasizing within me. ∎

PARTY, PARTY

Belinda McKeon

T here were a lot of regrets, but we didn't care.
We didn't want those people anyway. We didn't know half of
them. They were just names, stacked on a list, like signatories to a
petition for whales, or equality, or some doomed Saudi poet. We
had only invited them because we needed them to know; we didn't
actually need *them*. We were getting the ones we needed: Manvern
Clarke, and Marcus Kern, and Flynn Muldowney, and John Finnane;
Franklin Hodge, from Veto Dynamics, and Brick Garvin from
Garvin Solutions. Stefan Schlamme; Eric Leifert; Jean de Maigret,
over from Paris for the weekend. Sasha Vorven, and Róise James, and
Sian O'Hea and Izzie Neuwirth; we were getting a few artists, a few
writers, and P.J. Shanley, the composer, and Marie Fox, from Fox and
Foe. Tarot weren't coming, because Tarot were on tour in Australia,
but then Tarot were more popular in Australia, anyway. And someone
else would get the singing going; we'd bought enough drink to see
to that. On the wine, as on every other aspect of the night, Arlo had
guided us.

'Call this guy,' he said, giving us a card; it was for the sommelier
at one of John Finnane's restaurants. 'You don't tell him what you're
looking for. You tell him how it is that you want to feel as you watch
your guests drinking your wine.'

'Be the wine you want to be,' Brendan said, and, with a flutter of panic, we searched his face for sarcasm – but out of all of us, Brendan is the one most changed. He walks up to strangers in the street, telling them. He has been shouted at, spat at, even given a good beating one night near the old museum, but nothing can stop him. The party was his idea, although all of us had been wanting, for a while, to make it official: our newness. Our difference. Our *house*. The photo on the invitation was of our front door. Black. In our minds it had always been that colour, a non-negotiable slab of it – and matte, not glistening. Not interested in rain or in sunlight, not needing to cheerfully shine.

Arlo would be coming, of course. He would be a little late, because his flight would not get in until after ten, but he would be with us as soon as his driver got him into town. Still, we worried. What if there were delays? We considered calling our contact on the board of the airport, but there was too much, we knew, which could not be controlled on the other side. And Arlo would be with us. We knew that. *Trust in what you ask for.* Lesson Two, Module Four.

In the morning, the cleaners arrived. Two local women. One close to seventy, the fine bones of her face holding out against her ruin. The other younger, flint-eyed, her lips a sour twisting. Kate opened the door to them, and Gerrie stepped forward to give them their instructions, brisk and accusatory as Gerrie always knew how to be; she made it sound as though these women had themselves been the ones to dirty the bathrooms, to scatter the papers, to leave the eggs rotting in the shelves of the fridge door. They scowled, tying on their aprons and laying out their detergents. They knew well how to charge. But they would earn every cent of it. Gerrie would make sure of that.

We went back to what we had been doing. John took up his newspaper, underlining names, making notes in the margins. Kate got Ash, the child, ready for her trip to the woman's house, where she would spend the night; the woman has a name, of course, but for a long time now we have simply been calling her *the woman*, and it works; we always know who we mean. Ash is six, and the daughter of this house; she was, of course, the daughter of only one of us to begin with, but we don't believe in such distinctions any more. She had no interest in the party. She let Kate pack up her little rucksack, and she headed, with no questions, with no drawn-out goodbyes, for the door.

The cleaners handled, Gerrie went back to the guest list, marking it up one last time; we would all have final copies by lunchtime, and we were expected to study them until we knew them by heart. Martin went to his wardrobe, running his hands over the Lutwyche suit he would wear that night; the rest of us had looked up Lutwyche, and at first we were shocked at the prices but in the next instant we were proud, and we imagined Martin taking his jacket off as the night went on, leaving it where guests would notice the label, but we knew that Arlo would refer to this as scavenger thinking, and we were a long way beyond scavenger thinking now.

Laura did another check on the gift bags, making sure each one contained what it needed: the wisdom stone and the iodine pill and the specially commissioned book of poems. These days, to celebrate anything, you needed poems. That said, the specially commissioned poets were not actually, really poets; they had not actually, really, been commissioned; they were not actually, really people at all, but the inventions of Laura and John, who had written all of the poems in one night, letting wine and gin and whiskey hammer the lines onto their laptop screens. They had piled up a dozen or so books as templates, but they abandoned them after the tenth poem, or the twelfth; by then, they realised, it was just word, word, word, image, image, image, and a line break here and a triple indent there. *Coming/Going/Trying/Proud*, they called it, and on the back they put a blurb from a real poet, a poet whose name even the party guests would recognise, praising this volume of the youngest, freshest voices in Irish poetry, this bringing together of talents from all backgrounds, all ethnicities. Ash Editions, we called ourselves as publishers. It was a sweet touch, yes.

Maria went back to her tiny meringues, which would now absorb the poison of the cleaners' detergents as well as the dirt their lifting and swabbing and sweeping would disturb, but that hardly mattered. Karen went into town, to buy things she had always meant for us to have: certain types of vases, and certain books, and a bewildering and expensive lithograph for the hallway, an image of spindly train tracks disappearing over a horizon, or were the tracks a ladder? or was the horizon an end? and also she bought extra cosmetics and things for the bathrooms, and for the kitchen, a casserole dish, which came perfectly pre-burnished, looking as though it had already, many times over, fed hearty meals to a family of nine or ten.

We were ready. We'd been living in this damn house for years: bearing it, enduring it, piecing it into its proper shape, one floor, one room, one skirting board and light switch and length of copper piping at a time. We had not pulverised one another with copper piping over the course of that period; that was an accomplishment. Or maybe that was a miracle. And we believed in miracles. We believed in the grace and the beauty of what had been taught to us, about what we deserved and were entitled to have. We were blessed, that was the truth of it. We used that word without irony. We used that word without fear.

Ash led us to Arlo. We forget that sometimes; maybe we should be more grateful to her? But there is no sense in confusing the child. She functions best when her routines are kept neat. Like that day by the river; she was doing, that day, the two things it was her job to do, which was to sing and to offer roses. They were real roses, grown in the city's south gardens, and in the nearer suburbs; at night-time, we gathered them. When the time of year for roses passed, we would find other flowers, or we would give her other things: beautiful stones, maybe, or young animals. Those miniature squirrels you saw in the parks, or darting across telephone wires: could they be caught? Could they be persuaded to stay in a child's warm pocket, to look appealing and substantial in a child's small hand?

But thankfully, it did not come to the point of catching squirrels.

It was an evening in early summer, and Ash was working the faded walkway along the river, singing her songs of heartbreak and loneliness, and offering her fat, imperfect roses for sale, and from a safe distance, our own day of scrabbling and scavenging done, we were watching. She moved so perfectly; it was in her bones, the knowledge of how to do this. She wore a dark green pinafore, like a child her age might have worn to school, and grey canvas sneakers, and her hair was short. There had been lice in the springtime, and we had cut it; really, all of us who were long-haired ought to have given ourselves the same chop, but we did not, we reasoned, have the lush and able hair of a child. Hers would grow back. We held on to ours.

She was slight, but she was determined, that evening, weaving through the river crowds, singing in the language she had learned for this. The old language, the lovely one. It was so useful; people turned towards it and something deep inside themselves ordered them to give. Pennies, only, but we could use pennies. We stacked them on the kitchen table, and we divided them evenly. Or almost evenly; it was not always possible to be precise.

We were living, that time, with rats in the walls. And if they had stayed only in the walls, that would have been one thing. That would have been even, maybe, a comfort: we could pretend that the scratch of them was the sound of the radiators coming to life. But they did not bring us warmth and comfort, or even the dream of it. They did not stay only in the walls. They liked, in particular, that same table on which we stacked Ash's pennies. We knew we should not leave food there, our scraps and our leavings, but we were depressed. Eroded. The food was so awful – dug out of bins, snatched from the less visible shelves, the already-stale shelves, of the supermarket – that we had simply lost the will to clean up after ourselves. The rats were probably disappointed. The rats were probably having stomach problems as well.

How long had we been in the house then? Some of us said three years, but some of us said ten – but it could not have been ten. Ten would have been impossible. Ten years previously, life had been glorious. We had each had a house like this to ourselves – bigger than this – with the floorboards smooth and polished, with the windows open to the extensive gardens, from the lakes or oceans of which we commanded such views. But then the shame had come, and we had become only squatters, afraid of one another and yet in such need of one another that in the evenings, we would stand by the upstairs windows and watch for the return of those who were not yet home. Brendan had found the house, so Brendan got what had been the master bedroom, although it had no bed by then, and certainly no en suite; just a pile of blankets in one corner, and a broken toilet that he sometimes used anyway. The stench from that room was enough to keep the rest of us away; we lay down in other corners. In the kitchen, or on the landings, or, on summer nights, in the yard. Nobody could see us like this: that was what kept us going. Nobody but ourselves knew that we were living this way, so nobody who mattered could judge.

But then Arlo bought all the roses, and Ash ran out of song.

Her eyes sought us out, panicked, and we urged her, with our eyes, to keep going; to find something with which to entertain him, this man in the linen suit the colour of confidence; it was uncrumpled, and gleaming, and he balanced the stems on one arm now without hesitation, with no sign of worry that they might dampen the fabric, or stain it (in those days there were plenty of flowers dyed in over-bright colours being hawked on the streets), and with his free arm, he gestured to Ash to walk on in front of him, towards us. The child did not stir until he put his hand to her shoulder, and then she made for us as though that had been her intention all along. And when he reached us, Arlo dumped the roses over the railings into the junk-clogged river, and from the inner pocket of his jacket he took a business card, thick and sturdy, the same cream colour as his suit. The lettering was navy: ARLO PLUNKETT, it read, and a number. No description of what he was, this smiling stranger, of what he did. No explanation.

'The paper's made in one of the oldest mills still in operation,' he told us. 'Bohemian.'

'Come, Ash,' we said, attempting to draw the child to us from where she stood by his side, staring at us with a coldness and strangeness we had never seen on her face before.

'Ash,' the man said, resting a hand on her shoulder again, and she lifted her chin to him and gave a single, sombre nod.

'Ash,' we said again, allowing ourselves to sound more angry this time. 'Come on, now. Time to finish up for the day. Time to go home.'

But Ash met our anger with her own, and it was chilling on her young features, in her reedy voice. 'That place isn't home,' she said, and she turned away.

'Ah now,' her new friend said, holding her to him in a way that enraged us, but then he had released her, and he was bringing her to us, which made us bristle, but he reached out, and touched one of us – Brendan – gently on the sternum, and what Brendan told us later was that this touch did not so much send something through him as clear everything in him away. It was as though, he said – and even at this early stage, that first night back in the house, Brendan was using language we had never known him to use before, ways of talking which seemed to have come on him suddenly from the skies – it was as though a warren of spaces had opened up inside of him, and around him, pushing through his body so that the confines of his body ceased to matter. *Ceased*: the Brendan we knew would never use a word like *ceased*. It was the kind of word he'd jeer at, the kind of word by which he'd feel threatened: fine if it came as part of *deceased*, but by itself it would only be asking for trouble. And yet here he was, talking this way.

'First rule of telling a story,' Arlo said, 'is that you have to believe in it yourself. You have to believe it here, in your core.' And he tapped on Brendan's chest, once, twice, three times, the bone sounding back a dull attempt at protest, but Brendan's eyes unblinking.

And whatever it was that Arlo was doing to him, Brendan told us later, he would have done anything, anything, to have made it go on.

'Some kind of sex thing?' said John, who had not been there, and usually a suggestion like that would have Brendan flying into something savage, but no. He almost smiled. It had been nothing like that, he said, his voice soft and level. It had been, he said, a kind of force. A kind of, nearly, magic.

And to that, some of us said plenty, and some of us said nothing, just watching, waiting, though for what, we did not know. The child was in her bed by then. The wine Martin had found for us was almost gone. The moon was casting crystal-blue light upon the stones of the yard. And when we went out there to sleep that night, a knock on the back gate sounded, and when we opened it, we did not ask how he had known where we were.

W hat was shocking was how easy it was. Don't fall for the trap of asking how you could not have done this, changed like this, sooner, Arlo told us – but it was hard, sometimes, not to ask. Not to have these thoughts of wastage, this bitterness at ruined years. That we had suffered for so long, been deprived for so long; that we had fallen so badly, so devastatingly, out of existence, and yet this . . . salvation . . . had been within reach, within ourselves, all this time? Some of us thought of the rats, of how, at night as we tried to drop into sleep, we could not work out whether it was real or hallucinatory, that rustling at the bottom of our blankets, that quick, dry nuzzling on the skin of our soles. Some of us thought of the skin on our faces, and of how mottled it had grown, how coarse and lined. The mirrors in the house were fractured and blackened, but we could still glimpse ourselves, horribly aged, our features twisted by disappointment: another reason why Arlo's matinee sleekness was so difficult to bear. Some of us thought of our houses, the houses we had left behind, and of what had been in them, and whom – but these thoughts were better not to pursue in the first place, Arlo taught us.

He wiped us clean. The long room on the first floor became the classroom, and the table was cleared and scrubbed so that we could sit around it, and though the child's little table was by the high windows, never once did she look out, never once did she gaze down, distracted, by whatever was happening out there, by the whispers and grunts of the city. She gazed at Arlo, like we gazed at Arlo, and listened, and began to believe.

He taught us the things which were our birthright. That was all. Or, that was not all, for we studied with him for long months, each month more difficult than the last, but that was the core of it: that there was a reality to which we were entitled, and that to secure it, to claim it, all we had to do was to name it, over and over again. First we would believe in it, then others would follow, and then, Arlo told us, the world would be ours. The world as we wanted it. What did we want that world to be? How did we want it to look to us? To work for us?

A lie is only a lie when you are afraid of it letting you down: Lesson Three, Module Four.

A lie is not a lie when you decide otherwise: Lesson Three, Module Five.

Choose what you want and take it: Lesson Four.

And yes, there were so many others who had fallen as we had – but we were not them, Arlo taught us, bringing the heel of his hand down so hard on the table that it must have been painful, though his face showed no flinch of it, holding on instead to its constant, certain glow – we were not them, and they were very far from being us. And the ones who cannot muster, the ones who cannot climb; they are the ones who must be left on the highway, or in its shadow. They are the ones who must be gently abandoned, for the sake of moving onward. Not everybody can be special, he taught us. Not everybody can be saved.

In the kitchen, Maria's meringues were being gobbled. People had cream sticking to the corners of their mouths, sugared crumbs all down their fronts. The fridge was fat with bottles of champagne, and although we had hired servers, people were drinking it faster than it could be poured. Our hearts were pounding. Around us, eyes were so bright, so antic; to them, maybe, a night like this was only normal, but when we looked into one another's eyes, it was with giddy relief. We clasped one another's hands quickly, down low, hidden in the throng and push of the crowd, where no one could see, and it was a crowd, it had been a crowd within the first ten minutes. Their roar. Their faces, beautifully reddening. The swirled scents of their perfumes, like walking into an overthrown hammam. They spoke in code, but we understood every word of it; we slipped in and out of conversations as though these people were our family, except that we loved them, except that we wanted to hear everything they had to say.

'Consolidation,' Brick Garvin was saying to Manvern Clarke, who was nodding vigorously, 'Target, refinement, opportunity, and *bam.*' He slammed his fist into his open palm.

'. . . the original plans,' Sasha Vorven whispered to Róise James. 'And I also heard, some connection to the actual Romanovs . . .'

'The true worth, now, is in Windhoek,' John Finnane said to Millicent Rafferty and Elena Cave. 'Go there quietly, and dig in.'

'I got down on all fours,' Marcus Kelly told Flynn Muldowney and Franklin Hodge, who were helpless with laughter. 'What the fuck else was I going to do?'

In the hallway, Izzie Neuwirth was admiring the lithograph, although what she was really doing, she knew, was coveting it, but we had decided not to think that way, we remembered, so we took her praise for our taste, for our eye, and we turned it back onto her; we heaped praise on her last show, in the museum on the outskirts of the city, and on how momentous it had been, and how unforgettable – those astonishing seascapes, the way they drew you in with their depictions of the water, its textures, and then when you looked more closely you could see, and not unsee, the terrible wrecks. But in fact this was all based on a review we had read in the newspaper; we did not have time to see art, or indeed to try to unsee it. Still, Izzie turned from us, duly massaged, and we knew she would do us good sometime, and we were pleased with ourselves, and our next challenge was Tom Cassidy, who was heading up the board of the Excellence Initiative these days, and who smiled at us, beamed at us, as though he had turned from an altar and found us approaching, resplendent, to marry him; he kissed us, and shook our hands, and let us in on his secrets and made all the right noises when we let him in on ours. And, it was a divine house, a house of wonders, Ellen Kennedy, the designer, said; she went mad for the parquet, and for the mouldings, and for the library of first editions – at its centre an edition of *Ulysses* so early that it had barely been written at all – and for the view from the roof deck, over the mountains and the sea, over the passage tombs and shanty towns, over things which should have been impossible to have brought together in the span of just one gaze, but which had become more than possible; which had become ours.

A rlo was still not with us, and Brendan's nerves, we could see, were on edge. He was looking at his watch too often; he was casting harried glances towards every door. Gerrie gave him a sharp elbow in the ribs, which was not how it was meant to be – not the elbow, not the sharpness, not the suggestion of anything other than a happy, harmonious front – but it passed, and Brendan settled, and we could relax again. Along the walls, people were posing for the photographer from *Moment*. You had to pay for these photographers, they didn't just come; who knew?

On the landing, Stefan Schlamme and Eric Leifert were discussing a church they had been to, or maybe a church they had both heard about. 'Yes, the priest there is willing, but only during certain moons,' Schlamme was saying.

By the drawing-room curtains, Sian O'Hea was pointing out patterns in the fabric to Eric Pearse. 'Look, a hen,' she said, pointing to a spot that was perfectly white, as all of our curtains were. 'Look, a boat.'

'You pour hot water down the burrows,' Jean de Maigret was saying to Sasha Vorven. *Burrows* was not the right word for what he was saying; he meant *wormholes*, but they looked so good together, the two of them, that we did not like to interfere.

'Every one of them hand-painted,' Ellen Kennedy was telling Marie Fox. 'Even the seams. Even the places behind the buttons, the places no one could see –'

'Occasional phone calls,' John Finnane was saying to Manvern Clarke. 'Isn't it enough for them?'

'Some of them have to die,' someone said, but we could not tell who that was, and it could have been anyone.

B y Ash, Arlo was charmed, but no more than anyone would be by a child, by a quiet, watchful girl. He brought her things: the little plastic people she collects, so tiny, so detailed, made to fit on the top of a pencil or pen. We bought these people for her too, of course, or some of us did, but Ash preferred the people Arlo brought. It may have been that he got the rarer ones abroad, on his trips, in the toyshops there, or in the airports. She kept them in her room upstairs, in a tin box that was in the house when we came here. Her reliquary, Arlo called it. He always knows such words.

Her room was locked on the night of the party. We did not want people snooping in her things, or throwing coats across them, or fucking on them; a party, after all, is a party. Elsewhere in the house, people could do what they liked. We hoped, in fact, that they would do plenty. Not that we were hoping for debauchery, not openly at least; just a little light interest. Just something that would be spoken of afterwards. The whole pleasure of having the things we had lay in the power to declare that they didn't matter. The lithograph in the hall: how good it would look shattered on the parquet tile, and someone looking down at it in an agony of embarrassment. Better still, the *Ulysses*. What would the embryonic *Ulysses* look like, its pages as sodden as dishcloths by some '99 Château Haut-Brion?

By the fireplace, Marcus Kern was hitting on Kate, which was only to be expected, since she was the youngest of us, her hair blonde, her figure good. Kern was far gone, and looming over her as though about to collapse onto her, one elbow hinging on the mantel. And yet Kate, we could not but notice, was not doing what she needed to do. She was not smiling at him, or leaning towards him, or standing firm in the blast of his breath, which was infamous, and which everyone always wanted to step away from, but which you could not step away from, if you wanted the things that Kern could give. And here was Kate, now, actually backing away. And here she was, now, actually rolling her eyes.

'Oh, for fuck's sake,' Gerrie said, and swept over to them. She put her hand to the small of Kate's back, and she dug a fingernail into the bone, so that Kate spasmed, and tightened, and already Gerrie was smoothing and flattering Kern's ego, drawing it out nice and long. Kate, with Gerrie's warning touch still to her spine, took her cue and stepped in closer. Oh, the reek of Kern: whiskey and days-old trace of beef and vegetable; we could almost smell it from where we stood. But it was what we wanted. Kate had merely forgotten that.

Close to midnight, there was a commotion downstairs and we all rushed to the landing to investigate. We were glad of the chance to do so; Flynn Muldowney and Marcus Kern were debating the case of that girl who had, frankly, only made her own bed, and it was interesting, it was vital, but we had to escape. What we found was the poet, Manus McLoughlin, standing on our Eileen Gray telephone table and embarked on a dramatic reading of one of our specially commissioned poems. Someone had broken into the gift bags; there were wisdom stones and iodine pills in several hands and people seemed not quite capable of distinguishing the two, but this was not, we reminded ourselves, our problem. Manus stood like an auctioneer on our three-thousand euro sliver of chrome and beechwood, and he read:

> Stars in full darkness
> send out their signals
> Coming
> Going
> Trying
> Proud
>
> Our fathers took handfuls
> and made of them hayfields
> Coming
> Going
> Trying
> Proud
>
> Our mothers—

'This is horseshit,' McLoughlin broke off with a shake of his head, and as he stepped down, he put his foot through our table. The crowd roared their approval, or maybe they roared for more poetry; we could not tell, and we did not care. We had only wanted them to roar. Laura and John exchanged a thrilled look; they would be at it on the top floor within minutes, we knew. Arlo did not approve of us sleeping with one another, but Arlo – as a glance at Brendan's strained face would tell – was not here.

In the downstairs bathroom, someone had poured the Byredo hand soap down the sink, its gloop and shimmer clogging the plughole. In the kitchen, the casserole dish had been taken from the shelf over the hob and was being used by the smokers, their butts stubbed in hard so that the enamel darkened and stank. From the piano, someone had managed to tear the ivory away from a key on the upper octave, a clean, comprehensive tear; they would use it for a bookmark, maybe, or as a spatula for depilatory cream; we knew we were surrounded by people who did not have the mettle, or the discipline, to book themselves in for a monthly wax. Scraggy in all the places they still thought they could get away with. Under our suits and dresses, we were hairless and smooth.

Then the singing began. P.J. Shanley took control of the piano, looking delighted with himself, and everyone had something to offer, though their voices made the songs sound wrong. 'Slievenamon' like a battle cry. 'Don't Think Twice', a funeral dirge. 'Don't Speak', then, because the *don't* had put it in Róise James's head, and nobody knew where to look. 'The Lakes of Pontchartrain', a long whining, from Sian O'Hea, and 'Ol' Man River' from Brick Garvin, which was a bit rich – but no matter. It was a party. A party needed singing, and a party needed its guests, its happy, drunken guests, to sing along, and to congratulate one another, and this was why it was such appalling timing, not to mention such appalling manners, the way the child decided to appear at that moment. Or rather, the woman decided that she would appear, just as we were getting into the third verse of 'Galway Girl', just as the night seemed to be climbing towards its peak; by the drawing-room door, a fuss began, and it steadily grew, breaking its way into the singing, with people exclaiming, and nudging one another, and pointing, and then women putting their hands to their faces as though something terrible and mutilated stood there before them, and men looked surprised and unsettled, and P.J. Shanley's plodding piano chords came to a stop, and for fuck's sake, it was just a child with a bit of a nosebleed. It was just a child with a little bit of blood on her pyjama top and across her mouth. What did she mean by coming here at this hour? we demanded of the woman, who stood behind Ash at the door. She was wearing a winter coat, we noticed, a coat of a warmth that surely the night did not require.

'I don't know what to do with her,' said the woman. 'I can't stop it from coming. She's yours to look after, not mine.'

This was unacceptable, we told her. This was a party, we told her. She was interrupting it to bring us a child?

'The poor darling!' Izzie Neuwirth said, and she hunched down in front of Ash, but Ash, who was holding her little tin box of people, stepped back from her.

'Oh,' Izzie said, insulted, and she stood up again.

'She's getting it on the carpet,' one of the men said, and it was true, she was getting it everywhere, the rapid, angry flow; not just on the carpet but on the furniture, not just on the furniture but on the walls, and this was getting ridiculous now, this drama, and so we offered the woman much more than it was worth to take the child back with her, and we offered her double that, and triple that – in this, at least, there was some pleasure, some gratification, in letting people see what we could do – but it was no use. The woman wrapped her coat around her and made for the door.

'She's not mine to look after,' she said, tripping on the stairs. 'She's not mine.'

We looked at one another, aghast. The room was still in silence, the child's ragged breathing horribly audible, and even when people began to murmur to one another, and the noise level began to lift, we took no comfort from it. Ash was wearing her grey sneakers, we saw;

the ones she'd been wearing the night we met Arlo. They were too small for her now, her toes poking through the worn canvas.

'Give her some whiskey,' said Flynn Muldowney, and that gave rise to a moment's laughter, but then the heavy quiet came down again, and there was the child staring, bleeding, at the centre of it. Ice, someone said, or a towel, someone else said, or her head tilted well back to the wall.

'Like this,' Manvern Clarke said, stepping forward, and he took Ash's head firmly – some might say roughly – in his hands, and he pushed it back, and Ash's eyes went wide, and she dropped her tin box, her reliquary, and all the little people spilled, but the bleeding stopped. Or at least it slowed.

'Get her upstairs,' Gerrie hissed, and a couple of us went to her, and we took her out of there, and we left her in her bedroom with a towel, as had been suggested, and we came back downstairs. To cover the mark of her on the carpet, we moved one of the armchairs, and some people had questions, sure, but we were easily able to give answers, and before long, the singing took up again. And we finished what we had started, the 'Galway Girl', and everyone sang it, everyone shouted out and made defiant its chorus, and the wine turned out to have produced itself all over again, and the meringues appeared again with fresh cream and midsummer berries, and the paintings were ripped down and the first editions went onto the fire, but it didn't matter, it didn't matter at all, at all, and the little plastic people we kicked under the piano, or we danced on them, or we crushed them into Shenzhen dust, and we knew, now, that Arlo would not be coming to us; we knew, now, that we would not be pleasing him with what we had done. But we didn't need him, we realised. We were out on our own. ∎

STEPHEN SEXTON

The Butcher

It is the coldest noon in twenty years.
Outside deer are nowhere to be seen and inside
the radio spectrum fills up with sorrowful little packets of data.
Wasn't there a hart at the window yesterday, he thinks,
weren't there huge antlers.
What is there to be said of the unanswerable
phone ringing as it's been ringing lately
and of the village blue with snow, the flaked almonds of snow,
and there on the fold-up table folded out for once
the bowl of raisins she has eaten none of
for fear of unsettling her veil, today of all todays
and dawn coming so late last night it resembled mercy
until at last it came, resembling cruelty.
And what is there to say of all the hands and wrists
and forearms and the men shaking them and their regrets
into his palms like hucksters shilling counterfeits
and over whiskey nodding stories of times
they were right and other men were wrong
and how the pub was closed for an hour as a mark of respect
and chimney smoke over the village as though it was coffee cooling.

What is there to do with the sick pigeon sanctuaried against the
    woodpile
the beech tree was before the lightning brought it down which he
    claimed
with his beech-handled axe before the rest of town got wind of it
which he and the boy tramped back to the house with that last time.
And what can be left to say about the snow globe
in which all of this happens without taking away from the butcher
who must get to work grief or no grief if his neighbours are to eat
who must begin his work of opening up the way he will the newspaper
the coldest winter in twenty years
goes the headline and somewhere under the canopy
of the woods go deer shattering themselves against one another
with an architecture of golden blood and a rage they can't express.

SMILE

Roddy Doyle

B rother Murphy was about forty-five, but it was hard to put an age on adults. I didn't see them as younger or older than my father. All men seemed to be that age. But it wasn't the age; it was distance. They seemed far away, in another room or country. I didn't understand men. I wasn't alone. My mates were with me: all men were fuckin' eejits.

He was small, the same height as most of us. But he was wide. He came through the door sideways. His hair was cartoon black. It might have been dyed, but that wouldn't have occurred to us. He had a head and a jaw like Desperate Dan's. But he enjoyed his subject and he loved talking to himself in French at the top of the room. We, the pupils, never spoke French. We read and wrote but learning to speak wasn't on the curriculum. There was one day, he was at the board reading from the Inter Cert book. I can't remember its name but there was a skinny boy called Marcel – the book had illustrations – and he lived in a place called Saint-Cloud. I remember watching Murphy and thinking, 'He wishes he was there.' Murphy wanted to be a Frenchman. He wanted a beret and a Renault and a son called Marcel. He was happy in the book. I'm older than he was back then and I think I recognise it now: he was miserable. He was lonely.

And this violent man with the Desperate Dan head liked me.

I knew this – everybody knew this – because of something he'd said when I was thirteen, in first year.

—Victor Forde, I can never resist your smile.

It was like a line from a film, in a very wrong place. I knew I was doomed.

It was Friday afternoon and the sun was heating the room, spreading the smell. The school was right beside the sea and we could hear the tide behind the yard wall. It had been one of Murphy's happy days and we were at him to let us off homework for the weekend.

— Go on, Brother.

— Please, Brother.

—We'll pray for you on Sunday, Brother.

— *S'il vous plaît,* Brother.

He listened to us and grinned. It was a grin, not a smile. The word 'inappropriate' didn't appear until years later. But the grin was inappropriate. It was all inappropriate. He was being taunted and teased by a room of boys and he was loving it.

Then he said it.

—Victor Forde, I can never resist your smile.

There was silence.

It was late September. I'd only been in secondary school for three or four weeks. I hadn't even got the hang of it. All the different teachers, the size of the older boys, the violence and the constant threat of it. And the place itself was a maze. The trip from geography to science involved leaving one room, through another room after knocking and enduring the sneers and kicks of the fifth years; out to the yard, into another house, through what must originally have been the kitchen door, down a hall, and left, into a science lab that had a bay window with a view of the railway embankment and a huge fireplace. And thirty Bunsen burners. And a mad chain-smoking prick in a white coat leaning against his desk. Every day was exhausting. Exciting and upsetting.

The silent response to Murphy's declaration never ended. It did, eventually, but I hoped it wouldn't. There was still the possibility that he hadn't said it. While the silence lasted. But it ended.

Someone exhaled.

Everyone exhaled. Murphy had turned his back on us. He picked up his personal duster and rubbed out the homework.

— He fuckin' fancies him, Derek Mullally, sitting beside me, whispered.

Him, not *you*. Mullally shifted away from me. I wanted to pull him back. *It's nothing to do with me!*

— He's a queer.

—You're a queer.

— Murphy knows you're a queer.

— I wasn't smiling, I told them. I wasn't.

He'd been looking at me – Murphy had – all that time. *I can never resist your smile.* Since I'd walked in the front gate on the first day. The Brothers' house was beside the school. All the Brothers lived in there. Murphy must have been looking out the window of his bedroom at all the new first years as they arrived. And he'd decided that I was the one. There were boys in the class who still looked a bit like girls. Or there was Willo Gaffney, who said he had to shave every second day. There was Kenny Peters who had the scar on his forehead and was absent from school every time the circuit court came to the GAA club. I couldn't see why he'd picked on me. I wasn't like a girl or a man.

I'd no big brothers; no one had warned me about him. *Never smile back at him. Never get ten out of ten. Never get below five – don't give him any excuse to keep you back after the bell.*

I went into a school that was a row of big detached houses with black gates, a neat hedge and trees that looked as if they'd been planted hundreds of years ago. I'd walked out of our estate – there'd been five or six of us, together – where most of the trees hadn't survived, where some of the footpaths hadn't been finished. I hadn't been in there half an hour before I'd been hit, lifted by an ear and dropped, been called an eejit by the prick in the science lab because I thought he was pointing at someone else; I'd got lost and ended up in the senior yard and got kicked by a gang of lads who were okay, wouldn't have touched me, outside school. But I wasn't alone; we were all thrown, all the first years, all around the place. We suffered together and it was great. Then, last class, first day, before going home to my mother's questions, the French teacher, Brother Murphy, smiled at me, the first adult to smile all day, and I smiled back.

— And you are?

— Victor Forde.

— Victor Forde, Brother.

— Sorry, Brother.

— Have I had the pleasure of teaching any older Fordes? Any Defeats or Armistices?

— No, Brother.

I was pleased; I'd remembered to call him Brother.

He smiled again.

— Fine, he said.

He put a finger on my shoulder – it was just a strange little friendly, comical nudge – and pointed to a desk halfway down, under the window.

— You'll sit there.

— Thank you, Brother.

He smiled. But he'd smiled at all of us.

— Have I had the pleasure of teaching any older Kellys? he asked Moonshine.

— Yes, Brother.

— Oh, God help me.

He didn't mind us laughing.

— So, said my mother when I got home.

She was excited, young; she'd never gone to secondary school.

— How was school?

— Great, I said.

I meant it.

Her eyes were wet.

— I'm so proud of you, Victor.

She picked up my sister to make her kiss me, then made egg and chips to celebrate the occasion. I couldn't wait to go back in the next morning.

But then he singled me out. He'd smiled at us all, but he'd announced that I was the one whose smile he couldn't resist. I knew the others would kill me. I knew it as I began to understand what he was saying and what it meant. I knew the other lads would destroy me after the bell went and we were outside. And they did. They didn't even have to wait until we were outside the school grounds. The Brothers never minded violence. There was no point in trying to avoid it. I was surrounded, pushed.

—Yeh fuckin' queer.

— I didn't fuckin' smile.

A schoolbag – a Leeds United kitbag – was swung high and into my back. It hurt, but I laughed. The slaps became thumps. They were all over me. It wouldn't last; I knew that too. I was kicked, punched, spat on. For a minute. Only a few of the kicks really hurt, and the thumps were just to my arms and chest. No one kicked or thumped me in my face. The spitting – we did that all the time.

It was over. There was space around me. They'd drifted away. Only my real friends stayed behind. They laughed. And I laughed. I could breathe. It was over. Moonshine handed me my schoolbag. Doc picked my jumper up off the ground and walloped the muck off it.

I got sick when I got home. I put my mouth right over the bowl, so the vomit wouldn't splash too much. I waited in the bathroom until my eyes looked normal again. I put on my jumper, so my mother wouldn't see the bruises on my arms.

It wasn't over at all.

— Murphy's in his moods.

—We'll get the Queer to smile at him.

— Go on.

— Fuck off.

I was the Queer for forty minutes a day, three days of the week, and for an hour and twenty minutes on Fridays, right through first year. My mother never noticed how I started feeling sick on Thursday evenings, about once a month – I knew what I could get away with.

She never spotted the pattern. I was sick on Fridays but I ran to school on Tuesdays. We didn't have French on Tuesdays.

But staying away didn't work. I was miserable because I wanted to be in school. I wanted to be with the lads. And it didn't work because, nearly three years later, I was still the Queer and Murphy still couldn't resist my smile.

— Smile at him.

— Fuck off.

— Go on.

I didn't know – and I still don't know – why I changed my mind that day, why I decided to give up and accept the role. I don't think it was a real decision. I just felt it – surrender.

I put my hand up and clicked my fingers.

— Brother?

I heard Kenny Peters.

— For fuck's sake.

I was suddenly, unexpectedly, delighted. I was frightening even Kenny Peters. I did the click business again.

— Brother.

— *Oui?* said Murphy.

He turned from the blackboard to see who wanted him. At the same time, I heard the Canadian geese flying over the school, and honking.

— The geese are going back to Canada, I told him. Spring is in the air, Brother.

I wasn't looking at anyone else but I knew they couldn't believe what they were hearing. I was actually being the Queer, talking about spring. It was early April. I was talking about geese.

— So, I said. Any chance you'll let us off the homework tonight, Brother? To celebrate the departure of *les canards.*

— That's ducks, yeh fuckin' eejit, Moonshine whispered.

No one laughed.

They were watching the Brother at the front. They knew I'd gone too far. They waited for him to charge down to my desk, forehead first.

I smiled at the Brother; I grinned.

He looked at me, then away. He stared at nothing – at the wall beside the broken statue of the Blessed Virgin. The Brothers didn't know she was broken. She had a hole in her back. She'd fallen from her perch when Willo Gaffney had dragged the teachers' desk over to her during a free class, and climbed up and taken his lad out to make her give him a blow job. She fell off, sideways. We caught her, all of us, but Toner's knee had gone through her back. He'd been planking for the rest of the day because the left knee of his grey trousers was kind of dyed the light blue colour of Mary's plaster.

Murphy stared at the wall, then spoke.

—Take down the homework.

No one pleaded with him. No one spoke. The bell went. He left. We got off for Easter a week later and, the first French class after the holidays, a woman walked into the room. Brother Murphy never came back.

—Jesus.

—A woman.

— *Une femme.*

— Say no more, squire.

— *Une femme jolie.*

— Bleedin' hell.

It was unbelievable. Absolutely unbelievable. A woman had walked in from the world outside. The real world. We saw women all the time; our lives were full of women and girls. But this was the first time a woman had come into the school. The cleaners didn't count. We never saw the cleaners. Moonshine's mother was one of the cleaners but he was always home before she went up to the school.

The woman walked in. She put a bag on the desk.

— She's a teacher!

—Where's fuckin' Murphy?

— Dead. ■

CONTRIBUTORS

Colin Barrett grew up in County Mayo, in the west of Ireland. His story collection *Young Skins* was awarded the *Guardian* First Book Award.

Kevin Barry's most recent novel, *Beatlebone*, was awarded the Goldsmiths Prize. His previous novel, *City of Bohane*, won the International IMPAC Dublin Literary Award. He has published two story collections, *Dark Lies the Island* and *There Are Little Kingdoms*, and also writes for stage and screen. He lives in County Sligo.

Sara Baume is the author of *Spill Simmer Falter Wither*. She was named a Hennessy New Irish Writer in 2015. Her awards include the Davy Byrnes Short Story Award, the Rooney Prize for Irish Literature and the 2015 Irish Book Award for Newcomer of the Year. She lives in West Cork.

Tara Bergin was born in Dublin. Her first collection of poems, *This is Yarrow*, was awarded the Seamus Heaney Centre for Poetry Prize and the Shine/Strong Award for best first collection by an Irish author. She currently lives in the north of England.

Lucy Caldwell was born in Belfast. She is the author of three novels, numerous stage plays and radio dramas. Her debut collection of stories, *Multitudes*, will be published by Faber & Faber in May 2016.

John Connell is a producer and writer. His debut novel, *The Ghost Estate*, was published in 2015. He has just finished another, and is currently based in rural Ireland.

Stephen Dock is a French photographer. His work has appeared in *Le Figaro*, *Le Monde* and *Newsweek*.

Emma Donoghue is the author of *Room*, shortlisted for the 2010 Man Booker Prize, and screenwriter of its film adaptation. Her other works include *Frog Music*, *The Sealed Letter* and *Slammerkin*. 'The Wonder' is an extract from her new novel, *The Wonder*, forthcoming from Picador in the UK, Little, Brown in the US and HarperCollins in Canada.

Eamonn Doyle was born in Dublin. His debut photobook *i* was described by Martin Parr as 'the best street photobook in a decade'. The author portraits featured throughout this issue were specially commissioned.

Roddy Doyle has written ten novels, including *Paddy Clarke Ha Ha Ha*, winner of the 1993 Man Booker Prize. He has also written two story collections, a memoir, books for children, screenplays, stage plays and a TV series, *Family*. He divides his time between Dublin and confusion. 'Smile' is taken from a work in progress.

Doug DuBois's photographs can be found in the collections of MoMA, the Library of Congress and the Victoria and Albert Museum. His publications include *My Last Day at Seventeen*, published by the Aperture Foundation.

Leontia Flynn is the author of three poetry collections, the most recent being *Profit and Loss*, which was shortlisted for the T.S. Eliot Prize. She lives in Belfast and teaches at the Seamus Heaney Centre for Poetry.

Birte Kaufmann is a German photographer. She lives and works in Cologne and Berlin.

Belinda McKeon is the author of two novels, *Solace* and *Tender*. *Solace* won the Geoffrey Faber Memorial Prize and was named the 2011 Irish Book of the Year. She lives in New York and teaches at Rutgers University.

Siobhán Mannion has won awards for her short fiction and radio drama. She works as a radio producer for Raidió Teilifís Éireann and is currently completing a collection of short stories.

Mary O'Donoghue grew up in County Clare. She is the author of the novel *Before the House Burns* and the poetry collections *Tulle* and *Among These Winters*. She is an associate professor of English at Babson College, Massachusetts.

Sally Rooney was born in County Mayo. Her writing has appeared in the *Stinging Fly*, the *Dublin Review* and *Winter Pages*. She lives in Dublin and is working on her first novel.

Donal Ryan is from Nenagh, County Tipperary. His work includes the novels *The Thing About December* and *The Spinning Heart*, which was awarded the 2013 *Guardian* First Book Award, and the story collection, *A Slanting of the Sun*. He currently teaches creative writing at the University of Limerick, where he lives with his wife and two children.

Stephen Sexton's poems have appeared in *Poetry Ireland Review*, *Poetry London* and *The Best British Poetry 2015*. His pamphlet, *Oils*, was the Poetry Book Society's 2014 Winter Pamphlet Choice. He lives in Belfast.

Colm Tóibín is the author of eight novels, including *The Master* and *Brooklyn*, and two story collections. His play *The Testament of Mary* was nominated for the 2013 Tony Award for Best Play. He is the Irene and Sidney B. Silverman Professor of the Humanities at Columbia University.

William Wall is the author of four novels, two collections of short fiction and three volumes of poetry. His novel *This Is the Country* was longlisted for the 2005 Man Booker Prize. He translates from the Italian.